CONTENTS

All through history, people have worshipped God. In different times and places, their ideas of God have varied, as indeed they do today.

CHRISTIAN BELIEF

Christians are people who believe in one God, whom they call 'Father'. They believe Jesus of Nazareth was the son of God. He was born in Nazareth, in Galilee, about 4 BCE. His mother was a young woman called Mary and his earthly father was a carpenter named Joseph. They were both descendants of King David, the most famous Jewish king. For 30 years, Jesus grew up in Galilee and worked as a carpenter.

When his cousin John began to call people to change their way of life, Jesus began to **preach**. He gathered **disciples** around him. They were a group of close friends who stayed with

him to learn more about God. For three years he travelled in Israel with his disciples, preaching and healing. Finally, Jesus was arrested because he claimed to be the Messiah, and was executed by the Romans, like any common criminal. After he had been dead for three days he was reported to be alive again. Soon after, his disciples said they had been filled with the **Holy Spirit**, and they started to tell the world that Jesus was alive. He had always promised that God would send a helper, the Holy Spirit, to be with the disciples and to help them tell others the good news of Jesus. They went all over the Roman world preaching the good news that Jesus offered people a new kind of life. Christians now believe that Jesus is alive, that he does change people's lives and that he wants people to worship him.

WAYS OF WORSHIPPING GOD

A

B

C

D

CHRISTIAN WORSHIP

Worship is a way of communicating with God. Prayer is one way of doing this. It involves listening as well as talking to God. Christians believe that through worship and prayer they receive strength and guidance in their everyday lives. Prayer is for everyone, not just for monks, nuns and religious people.

MANY DIFFERENT WAYS OF WORSHIPPING GOD

Christians worship God in a great many different ways. These often include attending **church** services, where they sing hymns of praise to God. They also include reading the **Bible**, the holy book of Christians. It is read aloud in church services. Christians also read their Bibles at home, to help them understand more about God, what he is like and how he wants them to live their lives. There are also talks and lessons in church, which help people to understand more about their Christian faith. Sometimes a period of silence is included when people can quietly think and listen to God.

All over the world Christians worship the same God, but not all in the same ways. People of different nations often prefer to worship God in different ways. However, Christians never lose sight of the fact that they all worship one God, who sent his son Jesus Christ to share their lives.

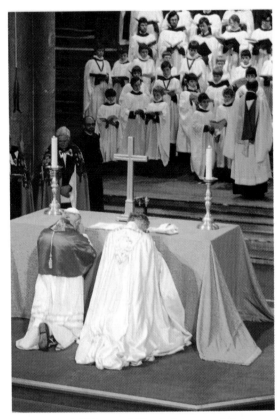

E The Archbishop of Canterbury and the Pope praying together

NOTES/DATABASE

Use the glossary to look up the meanings of the following words. Then use the definitions to make your own notes or suitable entries on your database.

Preach   Disciples   Holy Spirit

Church   Bible

1 **Quick quiz**

  a What do Christians believe about God?

  b From which king was Jesus descended?

  c What message did Jesus' cousin preach?

  d How long did Jesus spend preaching in Israel?

  e How did Jesus die?

  f What happened three days later?

  g What do Christians believe about Jesus now?

  h What do you think prayer is?

  i Make a list of the different activities which are involved in worship.

  j When would you expect a Christian to read the Bible?

  k Why do you think worship is different in different countries?

  l What do Christians never lose sight of?

ACTIVITIES

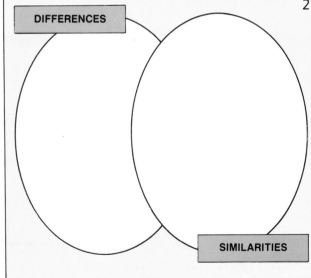

DIFFERENCES

SIMILARITIES

2 **The same God, different ways of worshipping him**

  a Describe what is happening in each of the pictures on these pages.

  b Fill in the differences and similarities in a chart like the one shown on the left.

  c What reasons can you think of for people to worship God in different ways?

  d Do you think the way that people worship makes any difference to the things they believe about God?

FURTHER ACTIVITIES

1 Survey some Christians

Ask one or more of your local churches if some of their members would fill in a survey for you. Here are some questions to help you design your survey. You will probably think of many more questions. You should make it clear that this survey will be anonymous.

Survey form

Tick correct box, please.

a *How often do you attend a church service?*   Weekly ☐   Monthly ☐
Occasionally ☐

b *Are you a member of the church?*
Yes ☐   No ☐

c *Are you a member of any other church organization?*   Prayer Group ☐
Guides ☐   Scouts ☐   Women's Group ☐
Men's Group ☐   Youth Group ☐
Other ☐

d *Which age bracket do you belong to?*
Under 11 ☐   11–16 ☐   16–25 ☐
25–40 ☐   40 plus ☐

e *How often do you read the Bible?*
Daily ☐   Weekly ☐   In church ☐
In RE lessons ☐   When I feel like it ☐
Never ☐

f *Which parts of the Bible have you read?*
Most ☐   Psalms ☐   Old Testament ☐
New Testament ☐   Gospels ☐
Epistles ☐   Very little ☐

g *How often do you pray?*   Daily ☐
Weekly ☐   When I feel like it ☐
Rarely ☐   Never ☐

h *Why have you chosen to attend this particular church?*   Near to home ☐
I belong to that denomination ☐
My parents went to this church ☐
I like the people ☐
I like the minister ☐   Other ☐

i *Is there anything you would like to change in your church?*
The minister ☐   The people ☐
The music ☐   The heating system ☐
The seats ☐   The organist ☐
Other ☐

---

2 Your results

When you have collected your survey forms, draw some bar charts to help you understand and display your results. If you have a suitable computer program for this, use the computer to produce a variety of ways to display your results.

What have you learned from your survey? Make sure that you show the results of the survey to the church you have chosen. They will probably be keen to display your work. They will also find it helpful in their work of helping people to understand more about the Christian faith.

3 What kind of things do people pray about?

a In small groups, discuss the kind of situations in which you think people might pray. Then make a list of the things you think people might pray about.

b Over the next few days, try to listen to a Christian service on the radio. Make a list of the things which are mentioned in the prayers. If you have prayers in your assembly at school, make a list of the things which the prayers have been about.

Compare your lists in answer to **b** with your group's list in answer to **a**.

4 A prayer

Now make up a prayer of your own on each of the subjects you have identified. You might like to use these for a display, or perhaps they could be used in an assembly.

Some people enjoy worshipping God in a small group where they know each other very well. Music may be led by a guitarist. The songs are often a way of expressing the love that the worshippers feel for God. People are able to talk about the Bible and how to apply its teaching in their own lives. Because there is a chance to discuss and ask questions, many people who worship in this way feel that they can take a real part in worship, and that this helps them to live according to Jesus' teachings.

5 For discussion

Do you think that many people want to worship God in the way described above?

6 Start a collection

Collect some pictures of different types of Christian worship from as many different countries as possible. Use these to make a display. Try to think of helpful ways of displaying your pictures. You might choose to group them by country or by the church that the Christians in the pictures belong to.

GET ON-LINE

If you have a computer link with other schools, try using your Bulletin Board to request pictures of different types of worship. You may get some answers from many different countries as well as many different denominations. Remember to include your address as well as your E-Mail number.

DATABASE OF CHURCHES

Begin a list, or a database if you have access to a computer, of the different churches you have contacted. You will need to add to this as you study worship and festivals. Work out ways of keeping in touch with the churches you contact.

WORSHIP AROUND THE WORLD

F

G

H

PEOPLE, NOT JUST BUILDINGS!

When the **New Testament** talks about the Church it doesn't mean the buildings . . . the early Christians didn't have any. It means the people who are believers in Jesus, who live in a certain town or area, or meet in one particular house. It is the people who are the Church.

The Church today is not just the building, either. At first the word 'church', or *ecclesia* in Greek, meant a gathering of people. The Christian *ecclesia* was the gathering of people who believed in Jesus and wanted to meet together to worship him.

In most villages in England, the skyline is dominated by the church building. It can be seen from miles away. Often it is an old parish church where people have worshipped God for hundreds of years. Sometimes the local church will be a modern building which can be used for clubs and playgroups, as well as for worshipping God.

Look up these references:
Acts 2:43-47
Acts 4:12-16
Acts 4: 32-38
These show what the early church was like.

THE EARLY CHRISTIANS

Buildings came later. The early Christians met in each other's houses. They sang hymns (songs about God and Jesus). They prayed, asking God for his guidance as well as for the things they needed, and tried to listen to God too. They ate together. Sometimes this was a special meal which they called '**breaking of bread**'. This was to help them remember the **Last Supper** which Jesus had with his **disciples** on the night before he died. They also tried to help one another and to share their possessions so that nobody went hungry. Paul, a leader in the early church, once collected a great deal of money from the richer countries of the world to send to Israel when there was a famine. When we read of the Christians doing these things, they are usually called 'the Church'.

BELONGING TO GOD'S FAMILY

The New Testament also refers to the early Christians as 'the household of faith' or 'the family of God'. Perhaps this is the easiest way to think of the church. To Christians, being part of the church is like belonging to one big family. The New Testament tells Christians that they should all care for each other as if they were brothers and sisters. This means spending time with other Christians in worship, and also trying to share their possessions so that no brother or sister is hungry. It means recognizing that brothers and sisters may live far away in other countries, and being prepared still to try to treat them as family. This is one of the reasons why the church is often involved in collecting money for charities, and with helping people in a wide variety of ways.

B We are the family of God

A Canterbury Cathedral

THE CHRISTIAN FAMILY NOW!

Christians usually worship in buildings which we call churches. They are also part of the group of people which we call the Church. Since the Church is intended to be a family, there are activities in most churches for all the members of the family. These are intended to help people grow up as part of the Church and to know more about their faith. Churches try to help people to try to live Christian lives, whatever their age group. There are activities for children, young people, adults and older people. As they grow up, there are opportunities to take on responsibilities and to help other people.

ALL CHRISTIANS ARE PART OF A WORLDWIDE FAMILY

Churches may belong to different groups of Christians, such as Anglicans, Orthodox, Roman Catholics, Methodists, Baptists, Salvation Army, Quakers and many others. All Christians are part of the worldwide family of God.

NOTES/DATABASE

Look up the following words in the glossary. Then use the definitions to make suitable entries for your notebook or database.

Breaking of bread   New Testament

Last Supper   Disciples

C General Synod in session

1 **Quick quiz**

a Where would you expect to see a parish church?

b Which Greek word means 'a gathering of people'?

c How does this definition help us to understand what Christians mean by 'the Church'?

d Make a list of the kind of things which the early Christians did when they met together as the Church.

e Why do you think that the early Christians met together in private houses?

f How do Christians try to show they are all part of the Christian family?

g Why does the Church now organize activities for all age groups?

h Name some of the groups of Christians who regard themselves as part of the worldwide family of God.

2 **Where are the churches?**
Put up a large scale map of your area on a notice board, or, if a table is available, pin a map to a large flat board. Then make sure you've got some long pins which you can use to make flags. You'll need paper in a variety of colours, and a fine pen or felt-tip to label them appropriately.

See how many different churches you can locate. Choose a different colour for each different denomination, and label a flag with the name of the individual church you have found. Place the flags on the correct spot on the map.

ACTIVITIES

3 Who is a member of the local council of Churches?
Ask one of the local vicars or ministers for the name of the chairman of the local Council of Churches. Make a list of the names of the churches which are members of the local Council of Churches.

Ask an Anglican vicar for the name and address of the chairman of the Deanery Synod (this is the meeting point for all the Anglican churches in the area). Make a list of the names of all the churches which are represented on the Deanery Synod. (You could write to the chairman to find out.) You could use a highlighter to show which churches are represented on each of these councils.

Council of Churches

Deanery Synod

4 Use your information

a Are there any churches which you located which are not on either of these lists?

b Find out whether there are any other committees or meetings on which several different churches are represented.

c Find out what kind of things are discussed or done by the local Council of Churches and by the Deanery Synod, e.g. local community work.

FURTHER ACTIVITIES

WORKING TOGETHER AS GOD'S FAMILY

1 Profile of a church

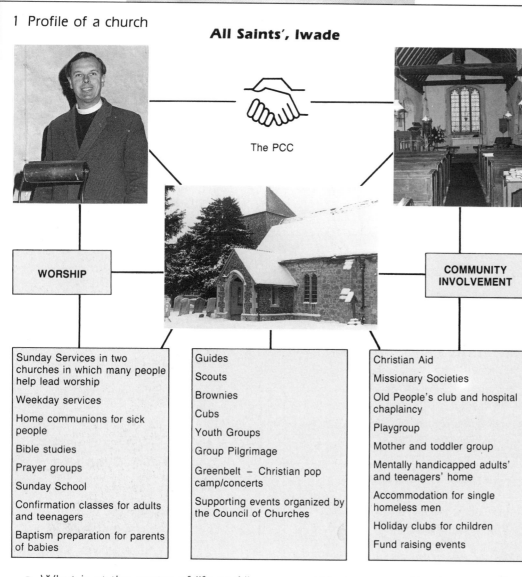

All Saints', Iwade

The PCC

WORSHIP

COMMUNITY INVOLVEMENT

Sunday Services in two churches in which many people help lead worship	Guides	Christian Aid
Weekday services	Scouts	Missionary Societies
Home communions for sick people	Brownies	Old People's club and hospital chaplaincy
Bible studies	Cubs	Playgroup
Prayer groups	Youth Groups	Mother and toddler group
Sunday School	Group Pilgrimage	Mentally handicapped adults' and teenagers' home
Confirmation classes for adults and teenagers	Greenbelt – Christian pop camp/concerts	Accommodation for single homeless men
Baptism preparation for parents of babies	Supporting events organized by the Council of Churches	Holiday clubs for children
		Fund raising events

a What is at the centre of life at All Saints'?

b Draw a chart which shows which groups of people might be involved in each of the activities on the lists.

c What might a child enjoy at All Saints'?

d What kind of things might a young person be involved in?

e What opportunities for responsibility do you think there might be at All Saints'?

f There is a lot going on at All Saints'. How do you think that all of these things get organized?

g Draw up a timetable of how you think a week at All Saints' might work out.

2 The Shaftesbury Society

The cartoon on the right was produced by the Shaftesbury Society. This was one of the societies for helping people founded in the 19th century by Lord Shaftesbury. He also founded the Church Pastoral Aid Society and the Shaftesbury Homes.

The following story was told by an old man who was found on the streets of London when he was a young boy in 1882.

I was sleeping on the streets in the East End of London as I always did. There were hundreds of lads who slept under tarpaulins and picked up what odd jobs they could to try and get enough to eat. One night a posh looking gentleman in a frock coat dug under the tarpaulin and pulled me out. He gave me some food, and took me to a big hall. Then he asked me whether I would like to have good meals and learn to be a sailor. I said I would, and that's how I came to join the Arethusa. It was a training ship in the Thames. I never knew whether the gentleman was Lord Shaftesbury or not.

Alfred

This is the kind of need which Christian organizations like the Shaftesbury Society and the Shaftesbury Homes met in the 19th century.

a Do you think Alfred was grateful for what the 'posh gentleman' did for him?

b How do you think Alfred's life might have been different if he had not been found by the gentleman?

THE Shaftesbury SOCIETY

CARING – IN JESUS' NAME

Please lend us a hand

COMMUNITY CARE

URBAN MISSION

SPECIALISED HOLIDAYS

SPECIAL EDUCATION

RESIDENTIAL CARE

SOCIAL HOUSING

c Look again at the list of things in which the Shaftesbury Society is involved. In what ways do you think the work they do now is similar to that done by the Shaftesbury Homes when Alfred was a boy?

3 Find out

a Find out about homeless young people in London now, and what is being done to help them.

b Find out about the life and work of Lord Shaftesbury.

4 For discussion

Look at the list of problems in the cartoon.

a Is it possible to help with so many different problems?

b Do you think it is just money which is needed?

c What other ways of helping people can you think of?

To find out more about Christian work in Britain write to:

The Church Pastoral Aid Society
Falcon Court 32 Fleet Street
London EC4Y 1DB

The Shaftesbury Society
Shaftesbury House 2a Amity Grove
London SW20 0LH

The Church Army
Independents Road Blackheath
London SE3 9LG

New Image Advertising Bureau
Any Street
London

Dear Sir,

We are planning an advertising campaign to assist the starving population of the Sudan. There is a great need for food and medical supplies. We would like you to design some posters which will tell people in this country about this need. Some of this campaign can be directed towards the Christian churches and should therefore emphasize the idea of the equality of all people and the need to distribute the world's resources fairly among all nations.

Yours sincerely,

5 Christian Aid

A man called Paul, or Saul, was one of the first Christians to organize a collection of money to help people during a famine. This tradition has continued throughout Christian history. Christians think that everyone on earth is a child of God and, as such, has a right to a fair share of the food and other resources of the earth. This is why Christians are always so active in collecting money and clothing for victims of famines and other disasters.

Make a list of all the charities you have heard of which collect money to help homeless or starving people. Now try to find out which of these are Christian in origin.

The poor haven't a share in the world.

Help the hungry, landless and powerless get fair shares.

Christian Aid Week May 16-21
P.O. BOX 100, LONDON SE1

CHURCHES IN ACTION WITH THE WORLD'S POOR

6 Design brief

Imagine you are the designer receiving the letter on the left. Carry out the work requested.

When you have finished your posters, use them as the basis of a display about world poverty and the ways in which Christians are trying to help.

THE CHURCH IS GOD'S FAMILY

Christians think of the church as being God's family. Some people belong to a Christian family group when they are born, others join later, when they have decided for themselves that they want to be Christians. The rest of the family always wants to welcome its new members, and has a variety of ways of doing it.

NEW MEMBERS OF THE FAMILY

When a new baby is born to Christian parents, they naturally want their child to be a part of the church family right from the start. If the parents belong to the Roman Catholic, Anglican, Orthodox or Methodist Church, then the new baby will probably be **baptized**, or **christened**. These are two different words for the same event. The word 'baptize' is used in the New Testament. People were either ducked under water, or water was poured over them. This was a sign that the things they had done wrong were washed away and forgotten about, and that they had become new people because of their belief in Jesus. It was the sign that someone had become a Christian, and that there was no turning back to the old Roman or Greek gods. The word 'christen' is a word used in the Middle Ages, which means 'to make someone a Christian', or 'to make someone like Christ'.

WATER IS A SIGN OF NEW LIFE

When babies are baptized, water is poured over their heads, and their parents make certain promises, for themselves and for the child who is being baptized, like the ones at the top of the next column.

- 'I believe in God the Father who made me and all the world.'
- 'I believe in God the Son, who redeemed mankind.'
- 'I believe in God the Holy Spirit, who gives life to the people of God.'

Alternative Service Book

- 'I turn to Christ.'
- 'I repent of my sins.'
- 'I renounce evil.'

Alternative Service Book

BELIEVERS' BAPTISM

There are some groups of Christians who believe that baptism is so important that it should only be for people who are old enough to decide for themselves that they want to be followers of Jesus for the rest of their lives. This is called 'believers' baptism'. The largest of these groups is the Baptist Church. Other groups of Christians who also believe this include Christian Brethren, Pentecostals and some of the House Churches.

A 'I gladly baptize you'

WELCOMING NEW MEMBERS

Naturally, the Christian groups who prefer believers' baptism also wish to welcome new babies into the family of God. They do this by having a service of Thanksgiving, and **dedicating** the new baby to God. This includes praying for the new child, and for the parents, and accepting, together with the parents, the responsibility for bringing up that child in the Christian faith.

B 'We welcome you into God's family'

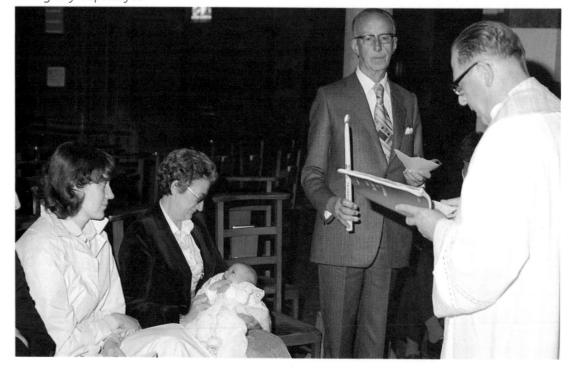

SAYING 'THANK YOU'

The Anglican Church has also introduced a service of **Thanksgiving** for new babies. This is for members of the church who believe that it is right to allow children the freedom of choice to be baptized when they are older. It is also for people who are not part of the normal worshipping family of the church but who, nevertheless, wish to say 'Thank You' to God for their new baby. It does not involve people having to state their beliefs and make promises in the same way as a baptism. The child can choose to be baptized later, if they have come to believe in Jesus for themselves.

C 'Shine as a light in the world, to the glory of God the father'

NOTES/DATABASE

Look up the following words in the glossary. Then use the definitions to make suitable entries for your notebook or database.

Baptize   Christen

Thanksgiving   Dedication

ACTIVITIES

1 **Quick quiz**

a Why do you think that Christian parents would want their children to be part of the Christian family right from the start?

b Which churches might the parents belong to if they choose for the baby to be baptized? Make a list.

c What does the word 'baptism' mean?

d What does the word 'christen' mean?

e Make a list of the promises which parents make when their babies are baptized.

f What is 'believers' baptism'?

g Name **three** groups of Christians who might prefer believers' baptism.

h How do members of these churches welcome new babies?

i Why do you think the Anglican Church has introduced a Thanksgiving service?

HOW DO YOU JOIN?

2 Investigate

a How did you become a member of the school you go to at the moment?

b How do you join the Scouts, Guides or the St John Ambulance Brigade?

c How do you join the local library?

D Members of God's family

3 Use the results of your investigations
Copy and complete the following chart.

4 For discussion

What reasons do people have for choosing to join a particular club or organization?

Organization	How to join	Reason for joining	Can you choose?
School			
Scouts/Guides			
St John Ambulance Brigade			
Public library			
Anglican Church			
Baptist Church			

BORN INTO GOD'S FAMILY

FURTHER ACTIVITIES

Many people think that baptism began with John the Baptist. Although this is part of the background to baptism, it in fact goes back a great deal further than that.

In the Old Testament, Noah, Abraham and Moses, as well as later prophets, were given signs of the relationship between God and his people.

At first, John the Baptist baptized people who wanted to show God that they were sorry for what they had done wrong in the past, and intended to lead different lives in the future.

John himself knew that this was only part of what baptism was about.

Read Mark 1:1–8 and make a note of what baptism is about for yourself. John said that the Messiah would baptize people with the Holy Spirit.

Later on, in the New Testament, baptism became the special sign by which people who wanted to be Christians entered into the agreement with God which showed that they were part of God's family.

FIND OUT MORE ABOUT BAPTISM

1 God and his people

Look up the references in the chart. Then copy the chart and fill in the sign of the relationship between God and his people and the part each of the partners played in the agreement.

Reference	Sign	God's part	The people's part
Gen. 9:11f	Rainbow	never destroy earth	be faithful to God
Gen 17:1–13ff			
Exodus 3:2ff			

2 Now read Acts 2:38

Peter says to the crowd that if they receive the sign of baptism, then God will do two things for them:
- Forgive their sins.
- Fill them with the Holy Spirit.

This is what Christians now believe happens when someone is baptized, and that is why they believe it is so important for people who are being baptized to understand clearly what it is all about.

3 The United Reformed Church

This Church accepts both infant baptism and believers' baptism. Contact the minister of a local United Reformed Church. See if you can arrange for them to visit the school to tell you more about baptism.

You will need to write a letter of invitation first. If you have access to a word processor, you could use it to write your letter. Make sure you explain carefully that you want to find out more about baptism in their particular church.

Before the visit, make a list of questions which you think you will need to ask. Here are a few questions to start you off.

CERTIFICATE OF BAPTISM

Rachel Elizabeth Mary Windsor

was baptized at

St. Helens and St. Giles

on

1ST May 1980

Rev. Peter Ratcliffe

Priest

The child has begun life as a Christian: it is the duty of the godparents to see that

Rachel

goes on according to this beginning.

a. How old are the people who are baptized in your church?

b. How do you prepare people for baptism?

c. Do you think someone needs to believe in Jesus before they are baptized?

d. What actually happens during a baptism?

4 Make a video

It might be possible for you to arrange to make a video about baptism, which explains the different views which each church has. This would be useful for other classes to use later on. You might like to include an interview with someone who is being baptized when they are about your age, as well as an interview with the parents of a baby who has been baptized.

E Film crew in action

TIME FOR SOME RESEARCH!

You could contact the local Council of Churches (you will find the address in your library) to help you find some information about baptism.

5 Collect together all the information you can find about:

a the history of baptism.

b baptism customs throughout the world.

c different attitudes to baptism in the various churches.

6 Now use your information

In groups, choose whether you would like to publish a booklet from

a the point of view of believers' baptism (only believers may be baptized), or

b the point of view of allowing the baptism of babies as well as adults (children of Christian parents may be baptized).

Now write and publish a booklet to help people who are considering baptism for themselves or their children. Make sure that it explains clearly what baptism is all about, and the responsibilities and privileges that it brings. Include suitable pictures and cartoons. If you have access to a desk top publishing system, you could use it for your publication.

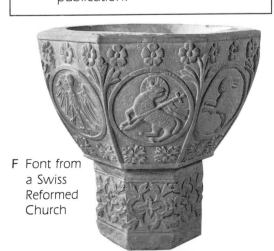

F Font from a Swiss Reformed Church

G Baptism of Constantine, by Puget

7 For discussion

If a baby is seriously ill, the parents may wish to have the child baptized.

a Why do you think the parents would wish this?

b What does this tell you about their beliefs?

8 Thanksgiving Services

Look back to the previous page for some information on Thanksgiving Services.

a What reasons can you think of for a couple with a new baby choosing a Thanksgiving Service instead of a baptism?

b Imagine you are the parent of a young child. Decide whether you would prefer a baptism, or a Thanksgiving Service. Make a list of the reasons for your answer.

SUNDAY

Sunday is a special day for Christians. It is the day which they set aside for worshipping God, with other Christians. They worship in a church or chapel, or sometimes they meet together in someone's house. Many churches have a Junior Church or a Sunday School for the younger members. This will be the time when they learn about the Christian faith. The children will have a chance to learn about Jesus in an appropriate way. They will be able to join in activities which help them to learn more about Jesus and about being a Christian. These may include music, drawing and painting, or drama, as well as reading and listening, and learning to pray.

CHILDREN'S SERVICES

Sometimes the children may spend part of the service in another part of the church, while the adults listen to a sermon (a talk which helps them to learn more about being a Christian). They will often join in a part of the main service.

A Roman Catholic first Holy Communion

Sometimes there will be a Family Service designed so that all age groups can join in together. Let's look at the Roman Catholic Church first.

FIRST HOLY COMMUNION

In the Roman Catholic Church, when children are about seven, they begin to be allowed some of the privileges and responsibilities of being full members of the church. This is the age at which they usually receive their first **Holy Communion**. It is a very important time in the lives of young Roman Catholics. They will receive special lessons which help them to understand more about being a Christian, and in particular about the meaning of Holy Communion, or **Mass** as Roman Catholics often call it. The first time they receive Communion is always very special. Proud relations come from miles away to be present. The girls often have special white dresses to celebrate this important stage in their lives and the boys dress in their best outfits.

THE MASS

Roman Catholic children will have attended Mass many times before they make their first Holy Communion. They will have seen the **priest** bless the bread and the wine and give it to each of the people in the congregation. The bread and wine represent the body and blood of Jesus, and Roman Catholics believe (along with many other Christians) that Jesus is present with his people in a very special way during this service. It is a great privilege to receive the bread and wine.

PRIVILEGES BRING RESPONSIBILITIES

Like all privileges, receiving Holy Communion brings responsibilities. In this case, the responsibility is trying to live life the way Jesus would want, and trying

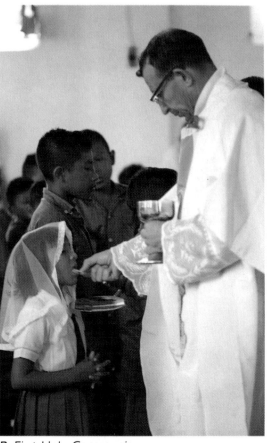

B First Holy Communion

to do the things he told people to do. These include being loving and caring, and doing what people know to be right.

Everyone fails to live up to the high standard which is demanded of a follower of Jesus. There are times when Christians know that they have fallen short and failed to behave in the way they know that Jesus would want. Christians call this 'sin'. Sin is really going your own way instead of God's way.

All Christians are encouraged to look honestly at themselves, and if they have done something wrong, to be prepared to admit it and to say they are sorry to God. Some believe that it is more meaningful and helpful to say this through another person. Roman Catholics regularly, in a formal way, **confess** to a priest what they have

C 'Lord hear us'

done wrong. He will then give them some advice on putting things right. He will assure them that God really does forgive people who have done wrong, if they are prepared to say they are sorry to God and try to lead better lives in future.

Shortly before a child receives Holy Communion for the first time, they will have made their first **Confession**. The Church recommends that every practising Roman Catholic makes their confession at least three times a year, and also receives Holy Communion at least three times a year. Most Roman Catholics will actually receive Communion a great deal more often.

D Serving God

What is Sin? Some Christian answers

- Going your own way instead of God's way.
- Putting yourself first.
- Anything which hurts God or hurts someone else.

A pattern of confession

I confess to God Almighty, the Father, the Son, and the Holy Spirit, in the sight of the whole company of heaven, and to you, Father, that I have sinned in thought, word and deed, through my own fault . . .

NOTES/DATABASE

Look up the following words in the glossary. Then use the definitions to make suitable entries for your notebook or database.

Holy Communion

Mass

Priest

Confession

ACTIVITIES

1 **Quick quiz**

a Which day is set aside by Christians for worshipping God?

b How do many churches help their young members to learn more about their faith?

c What kind of activities might there be to help young people to learn more about God?

d How old are Roman Catholic children when they receive their first Holy Communion?

e How have the children been prepared for their first Holy Communion?

f In what ways do adult Roman Catholics show children that first Holy Communion is a very special day?

g When do Roman Catholics believe that Jesus is with them in a very special way?

h What are some of the responsibilities of Christians?

i What is it called when Christians fail to live up to the high standards which Jesus set?

j How do Roman Catholics say 'sorry' to God for the things they have done wrong?

FURTHER ACTIVITIES

1 Find out

a You might go to a Roman Catholic school, or a Church of England school, or one without a specific religious link. What other schools are there in your area?

b What differences are there between schools which have a religious link and other schools?

c Find out some details about the similarities and differences between the schools.
Perhaps it would be possible to invite some pupils from another type of school to tell you about their school.

d Design a chart which shows the similarities and differences between the schools. If there are any religious differences, display them on your chart. The example shown will help you.

Differences and similarities between a comprehensive school and a Roman Catholic School.

St. Joseph's Convent	Shakespeare Comprehensive
Nuns as teachers	No nuns
School uniform	School uniform.

Ask the pupils from a Christian school how they were prepared for first Holy Communion, and what it was like. You might like to tape their replies. Many of them will have photos and certificates. Ask them if you can see them, and perhaps photocopy them to make a display.

The video about the Roman Catholic Church in the series 'Believe it or not' has a good section on first Holy Communion. If you have access to a video digitizer, use some shots from this video as part of your display.

E A Roman Catholic school

2 What do you think?

Roman Catholics believe that it is important to allow children to have a real experience of worship at a very young age. They believe that this will help them to live as Christians throughout their lives. Many Roman Catholic boys, from the age of about nine onwards, become 'altar boys' or 'servers' and assist the priest at Holy Communion.

I always loved being an altar boy. I didn't mind having to get up early to go to church because it always made me feel close to God when I helped at the service in this way. I didn't even mind too much when the boys at school teased me for wearing a cassock. Somehow it made me feel good to help in this way.

Alex, aged 14.

Roman Catholics also encourage children to take part in services by reading the lessons (from the Bible) and leading some of the prayers.

a Do you think it is a good idea to encourage children to take a real part in worship by receiving Holy Communion?

b What reasons do you think a young Roman Catholic boy might have for choosing to be an altar boy?

c In what ways do you think children should help in leading worship?

Section of the Communion service	Child	Teenager	Adult	Priest
Leading music Serving Reading Bible aloud Leading prayers Presenting the bread and wine Taking the collection Sermon Blessing the bread and wine Giving the bread and wine to the people				

3 Copy and complete the chart opposite
Place a tick in the column for the group of people you think could lead that part of the Communion service.

Read 1 Corinthians 12:27–30. What does this tell Christians about their place in God's family?

4 Find out
Which parts of the service are only ever led by the priest? What reasons can you think of for this?

PRIVILEGES AND RESPONSIBILITIES

5 Something to think about

a What do you ever feel bad about?

b Are there times when you know that you have done something wrong?

c Do you think it would help you to put things right if you could talk it over with someone who wasn't involved?

d Do you think it helps to be told that you are forgiven?

Has this ever happened to you?

I'm sorry, I won't do it again.

(Five minutes later)

Oh no, I've done it again.

F Hearing confession

What makes the difference to make this happen:

I'm sorry, I won't do it again!

and to know, inside yourself, that you really are sorry enough to never do that thing wrong again?

Christians believe that the difference comes when people know, deep down inside, that God has forgiven them, and that he goes on loving them whatever they do wrong.

6 Research

Look up the Bible references in the shaded box.

> *1 John 1:8–9*
> *Mark 2:10*
> *Isaiah 1:18*

USE the information

How might these verses help a Christian to understand that God is loving and forgives people who are really sorry when they have done something wrong?

A man called St Augustine of Hippo once said, 'Love God and do what you like.' What he meant was, that if you love God, what you like to do will always be what God wants you to do.

7 For discussion
How far do you agree with St Augustine?

Who was St Augustine of Hippo?

He was a bishop in North Africa in the third century.

HOLIDAY CLUBS

Many churches hold holiday clubs for their young members. These will often take place during a week of the summer holidays. There will be a theme for the week, with perhaps a set of videos which tell a story with a Christian message. This will be accompanied by games and activities. There will be a chance for the younger members of the Christian family to learn about Jesus in a way which is fun. Music, art and drama often play a large part in holiday clubs. Very often, the helpers at the holiday club will be teenagers. It is a chance for them to tell younger people about the Christian faith as well as an opportunity for them to help people.

Christians have always thought that holidays were important. The word 'holiday' came from the phrase 'Holy Day'. These were the special days on which particular events in the life of Jesus were specially remembered. It is not surprising, therefore, that Christian churches often have special events during the 'holidays'.

A   Holiday Club activities

BECOMING A FULL MEMBER OF GOD'S FAMILY

When Baptist and Pentecostal young people are teenagers, they often come to the decision that it is time they were recognized as grown up members of the church. These young people who have decided that they believe in Jesus and want to follow him for the rest of their lives, are baptized.

B

In the Baptist and Pentecostal churches (as well as some others) this is by **full immersion**. This means that they are ducked right underneath some water in a pool in a church, called a baptistry, or in a river.

Usually these young people will have attended a series of lessons in which they will have learned more about being Christians. These will have given them the opportunity of finding out whether they really wish to be baptized and to promise to be one of Jesus' followers. They will also have attended that church for some time.

At the baptism, the people who are about to be baptized usually have the chance to say why they have decided to follow Jesus, and to promise publicly to follow him.

At around the same time, they will also begin to share in the Communion service. This is another part of being a grown up member of the church.

CONFIRMATION

Anglican young people have the opportunity to be **confirmed**. This is really the second half of baptism. At confirmation, a person makes for themselves the promises which their parents and godparents made for them when they were baptized. Like the Baptist and Pentecostal young people, they attend some classes to find out more about the Christian faith. If they were not baptized when they were babies, then there is the opportunity to be baptized and confirmed at the same time. Young people who have experienced this often find it a very exciting occasion.

At a confirmation, the people who are going to be confirmed kneel in front of the bishop, who puts his hands on their heads as a sign that he is passing the gift of the Holy Spirit to them in the same way as it was received by the Christians in the New Testament. Christians believe that they receive the gift of the Holy

Spirit at baptism (or when baptism is completed, at confirmation). They believe that this is the way in which Jesus is alive with his people, so that he can guide them in their everyday lives.

SHARING IN THE FAMILY MEAL

After they have been confirmed, Anglican young people begin to receive Holy Communion. Together with all the full members of the church, they can share in the bread and wine which is given to the people during the service. This service can be thought of as the family meal which members of God's family share in whenever possible. Like Roman Catholic youngsters, many young Anglicans become servers, or choir members, or begin to help in the church in other ways, such as assisting with the Sunday School.

At about 14 or 15, Roman Catholic young people are also confirmed. Many Roman Catholics regard confirmation as the moment when they take on the adult responsibilities of being a member of the church.

Confirmation Prayer

Defend O Lord, these your servants with your heavenly grace, that they may continue yours for ever, until they come to your everlasting Kingdom.

Amen

NOTES/DATABASE

Look up the following words in the glossary. Then use the definitions to make suitable entries for your own notebook or database.

Full immersion

Confirmation

I was confirmed when I was 16. It was a very exciting occasion, as I was baptized at the same time. I decided to be confirmed because I believed in Jesus. I wanted to do something public to show my friends that I believed in him. At 16, when lots of my friends were teasing me for going to church, this was quite difficult.
The baptism will always stick in my mind. When the bishop made the sign of the cross on my forehead it felt indelible. A few minutes later, I knelt before the bishop as he prayed that God would fill me with the Holy Spirit. Somehow, I knew that I was different after the confirmation because I had found the courage to show publicly what I believed.

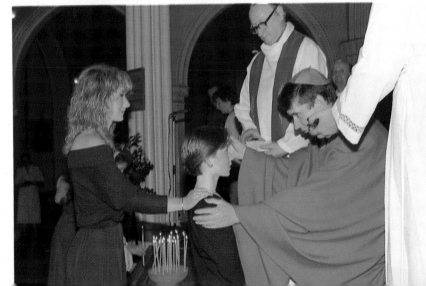

C Becoming a full member of God's family

ACTIVITIES

1 **Quick quiz**

a Why is it not surprising that Christians have special events for young people during the holidays?

b What kind of activities might take place at a holiday club?

c What would happen during a baptism by full immersion?

d How might a young person find out whether they really wanted to be baptized?

e What else will happen at about the same time as young Baptists and Pentecostals are baptized?

f What opportunity do Anglican young people have to renew the promises made at their baptism?

g How do Anglican young people prepare for confirmation?

h What happens at a confirmation?

i What gift do some Christians believe that they receive at baptism or when baptism is completed, at confirmation?

j When are Anglican young people allowed to receive Holy Communion?

k What other ways do some of them choose for helping in the church?

l How old are Roman Catholic young people when they are confirmed?

FURTHER ACTIVITIES

1 **Find out about holiday clubs**
Some people in the group may have attended holiday clubs. They may be able to give you some ideas. Others may have helped at a holiday club and be able to give some good advice, as well as sharing their experience with you.

You might like to ask a local vicar or minister to tell you about the holiday clubs which his church has run.

Here are three organizations which specialize in producing materials to help churches run holiday clubs. They will supply you with information.

a Scripture Union
130 City Road
London EC1 2NJ

b The Church Army
Independents Road
Blackheath
London SE3 9LG

c The Church Pastoral Aid
Society
Falcon Court
Fleet Street
London EC4Y 1DB

D Learning with the Scripture Union

Helping at Holiday Club was good fun. I enjoyed the company of younger children. There were children of all ages from four to eleven. It was very noisy and very hard work. All the leaders had been to planning meetings so we knew what was going to happen. I enjoyed the videos, and although they were intended for younger children, I felt that I learned a lot too. The games were very chaotic and occasionally some of the younger children cried, especially when they fell over.

Most of the kids enjoyed the music. We sang some funny songs, which made the helpers laugh. The children really loved them. On the last day, there was a picnic and a performance of some of the songs and plays for the parents. Lots of people had made models, and these were on display for the parents as well.

If I get the chance I will help again next year.

Matthew Aged 15

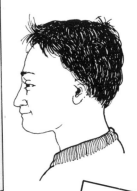

Plan a
Holiday
Club

ST MARY'S HOLIDAY CLUB

presents

On Fire!

A week of adventures every morning

| VIDEOS | GAMES | BIBLE STORIES |
| MUSIC | ART | DRAMA |

Lots of fun for everyone!

9 a.m. to 12 noon

Every morning next week in the Parish Hall

Our Holiday Club was held at the church hall. It was in one week in August. Each morning it was open from 9.30 a.m. until 12.30 p.m. There was orange juice and biscuits in the middle. First of all we watched a film each day. This year it was about a garage called Top Gear Motors. The first day it was about a car which didn't like the new foreign car. They had lots of quarrels but in the end they all ended up as good friends because they realised they were all much the same under the bonnet. I suppose it was trying to show us how we should all be friends. The last one was about Fandango, the old car who had to have a new engine. This one was telling us that we sometimes needed to change. We learned lots of new songs. Some of them were a bit silly, like "If I were a butterfly, I'd thank you God for giving me wings". But we still enjoyed them. There were lots of games and things to make and on the last day there was a picnic. It was good fun, and came just at the right time, in the middle of the holiday.

Gemma aged 10

2 Now it's your turn.
Find out, from one of the addresses on the left hand page, about some suitable materials for a holiday club, and start to plan your own.

You will need to:
- Arrange dates.
- Work out how many children you will expect.
- Work out how many helpers you will need.
- Work out how much orange juice and how many biscuits you will need.
- Work out how much it will cost to run the holiday club.

Decide whether to charge the children, or pay for it out of church funds.

Finally – what is the real reason for running your holiday club?

Time	Activity	Things needed
9.00	Registration	Database
9.15	Games	Rounders equipment
9.45	Worship	Guitars, words of songs, percussion
10.00	Video	Tape, video player
10.30	Orange juice and biscuits	Refreshments
10.45	Art/drama	Paint, glue, paper, dressing-up box
11.15	Music workshops/model making	
11.45	Final worship	Guitars, music and words

Now:
- Plan your timetable, like the example above.
- Design posters.
- Design invitations – use a desk top publishing system for this.
- Plan your daily activities.
- Set up a database which would help you keep track of the children who would attend.

A local church might be grateful for all your hard work. This might be a way in which you could help your local community! Why not give it a try?

A FAMILY MEAL

Family meals are often an important part of family life. People feel that they belong when they share a meal together. The church family also has a 'meal' in which all its members share. This is the **Holy Communion** or **Eucharist**. Roman Catholics also use the word 'Mass' and Christian Brethren often prefer the term 'Breaking Bread' or 'The Lord's Supper'. Some Christians, including the Salvation Army and the Quakers (Society of Friends), do not celebrate the Eucharist.

DO THIS IN REMEMBRANCE OF ME

The reason for this meal goes right back to Jesus himself. On the night before he died, Jesus ate a meal with his friends. Because this was the last meal before the **Crucifixion**, we call this the **Last Supper**.

After the meal was over, Jesus took a loaf of bread and broke it in pieces. He gave it to each of his disciples and said, 'This is my body, which will be broken for you, eat this in memory of me.' Then he took a cup full of wine, and passed it round to each of them, and said, 'This is my blood which shows that there is a new agreement between God and man, drink this in memory of me.'

Jesus told his disciples to go on doing this in memory of him and, for many, this has become the central part of Christian worship. When Christians take part in this family 'meal', many of them believe that Jesus is really with them in a special way. Christians believe that Jesus is alive and with them at all times, but especially in this service.

Soon after the **Resurrection**, the disciples began to meet to break bread. This meant that they shared in a common meal. Paul writes, in 1 Corinthians 11, about the night when Jesus first told his disciples to 'Do this in remembrance of me'. Paul thought it was important that they did not simply come to eat and drink, but to worship Jesus.

FAMILIES CARE ABOUT ONE ANOTHER

Christians feel that they are all part of the worldwide family of God, sharing in the family meal. This means that they have a responsibility to all other Christians and in fact to all other people. Part of worship is to pray for other people, and this also means doing something practical towards helping others. It is often the shared meal of Communion which makes Christians

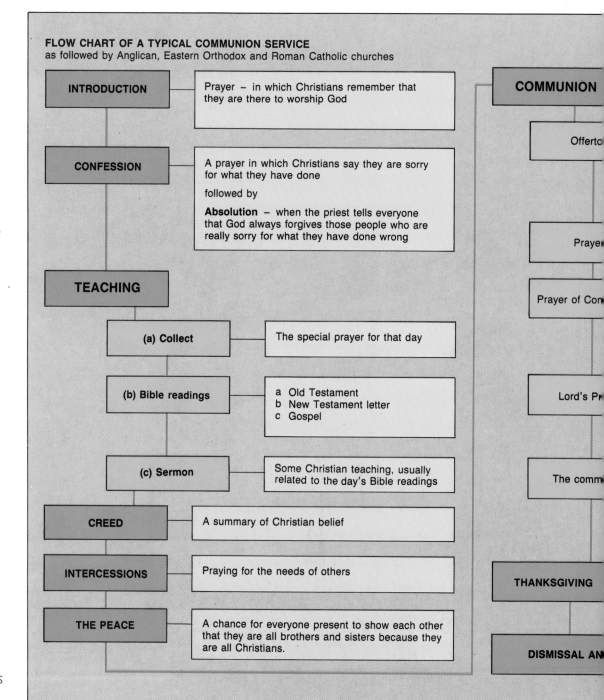

FLOW CHART OF A TYPICAL COMMUNION SERVICE
as followed by Anglican, Eastern Orthodox and Roman Catholic churches

INTRODUCTION — Prayer – in which Christians remember that they are there to worship God

CONFESSION — A prayer in which Christians say they are sorry for what they have done

followed by

Absolution – when the priest tells everyone that God always forgives those people who are really sorry for what they have done wrong

TEACHING

(a) Collect — The special prayer for that day

(b) Bible readings —
a Old Testament
b New Testament letter
c Gospel

(c) Sermon — Some Christian teaching, usually related to the day's Bible readings

CREED — A summary of Christian belief

INTERCESSIONS — Praying for the needs of others

THE PEACE — A chance for everyone present to show each other that they are all brothers and sisters because they are all Christians.

COMMUNION

Offerto

Prayer

Prayer of Con

Lord's Pr

The comm

THANKSGIVING

DISMISSAL AN

realize that they have a responsibility to do something about the starving people in the Developing World. Christian Aid, Cafod, Tear Fund and many others are Christian responses to suffering in which Christians try to work out exactly what it means to share in a common meal. Clearly it can have no real meaning unless they are also prepared to do something positive towards providing meals for others.

VARIETY

Some Communion services are quiet, reverent services in which an individual can feel closer to God. Others emphasize the family nature of being a Christian. People join in hymns together, and praise God in a cheerful, family way. This often includes children and young people who are too young to be allowed to receive the bread and the wine. Often these young people will go with the adults to the front of the church to receive a **blessing** from the priest or minister. Sometimes they will take part in leading music by singing in a choir or music group or reading the Bible or leading prayers.

AT THE CENTRE OF CHRISTIAN LIFE

Many Christians find a special joy in worshipping God in the Communion Service. It becomes a central part of their lives on which they depend for maintaining their relationship with God. Through it, they are more aware of God's love and his care for the world. They are also more aware of their responsibility to do the work in the world to which they believe God has called them.

Bread and wine are brought to the priest and prepared for communion.

There is often a money collection which is brought to the priest and offered to God for the work of the church.

These remind Christians that they are in God's presence

During this prayer, the priest uses the words Jesus used at the Last Supper (see 1 Corinthians 11:23) when he told his disciples to eat the bread and drink the wine in memory of himself.

The family prayer of the church in which Christians show that they are God's family in a special way when they are gathered for the family meal.

The most important part of the service, when all full members of the church receive the bread and the wine at the altar. Younger members also go to the front of the church to receive a special blessing.

Final prayers thanking God for the communion, and promising to do God's work in the world in the coming week.

G BY THE PRIEST

NOTES/DATABASE

Look up the following words in the glossary. Then use the definitions to make suitable entries for your notebook or database.

Eucharist   Crucifixion

Resurrection   Blessing

ACTIVITIES

1 **Quick quiz**
   a Make a list of some of the names used for the family meal which Christians share.

   b What was the Last Supper?

   c What did Jesus do after the meal was over at the Last Supper?

   d What do many Christians believe happens when they share in the family meal of the church?

   e Look up 1 Corinthians 11:23ff. What does Paul say happened that night?

   f Why do you think Christians might feel more tuned in to God during this service?

   g How do you think the Eucharist helps Christians to feel part of the worldwide family of God?

   h How does the Eucharist help Christians to respond to suffering?

   i Make a list of the ways in which some Christians try to help hungry people wherever they are in the world.

   j Why do you think that Communion services have such a variety of different atmospheres?

   k How can young people take part in the service?

   l Why do you think that the Communion service becomes a central part of worship for many Christians?

LIVING IN GOD'S FAMILY

1 Read what Gill and Carol have to say about the Communion service

   a Do you think they each attend church every week?

   b What is important about the service to Carol?

   c What do you think Gill finds important?

   d Why do you think Gill used the words from the Anglican Service of Communion to explain what she felt about the service?

The way I see it!

a Carol   (shortly after she was confirmed)

*Whilst I do not feel that this is **the** most important part of the service (all aspects are of equal importance in my view), it is a poignant time with a sense of calm, forgiveness and the chance to begin again.*

The action of moving to the altar rail, and kneeling there, serves to emphasize the need to come to God to ask for his forgiveness in the awareness that it will be freely given in love.

FURTHER ACTIVITIES

b Gill   (a Christian for many years)

'. . . As we eat and drink these holy gifts in the presence of your Divine Majesty, renew us with your Spirit, inspire us with your love, and unite us in the Body and Blood of your Son, Jesus Christ our Lord.'

These words, taken from the Order of Holy Communion in the Anglican Church, seem to sum up for me what the Eucharist means.

It is an oasis to which I go for refreshment at the end of each week. It is also the beginning of the week, a peaceful time during which I pause and reflect and 'recharge my batteries'. To continue the metaphor, the bread and wine top up my batteries and keep my spiritual engine running.

2 Something to think about

   What do you think is the main reason why Carol and Gill attend the Communion service?

   Do you think it helps them in the rest of their lives?

CHOOSING HYMNS AND READINGS

3 Look carefully at the flowchart of the Communion service (on the previous page)

   Many Communion services have a number of hymns during the service, and some other parts, like the Creed, may also be sung. You might be able to borrow a tape of a musical Communion service. *The King of Glory*, by Betty Pulkingham, sung by the 'Fisherfolk' is a good example of a modern setting.

   a Choose *six* hymns for a Communion service. Many hymn books will have a special section for Communion hymns.

   b Now select some Bible readings. You will need one from the Old Testament, one from one of the New Testament Letters and one from one of the Gospels (Matthew, Mark, Luke or John). If you have access to an Alternative Service Book (the Anglican Prayer Book) you might like to select the readings for next Sunday. Make sure the readings have a common theme, and help people to learn more about Christian life.

   c Now redesign the flowchart of the Communion service, putting in the hymns and readings of your choice.

A 'All things come from you, O Lord, and of your own do we give you'

4 Free Church Communion services

The Free Churches, including Methodists, Baptists, United Reformed Church and many others, often have less formal Communion services. They will often take place after the main family service.

Find out all you can about Communion services in a Baptist, Methodist or United Reformed Church.

B 'The Peace of the Lord be always with you'

THE CHRISTIAN BRETHREN

The Christian Brethren call their Communion service **the Breaking of Bread**. There is no set pattern of worship, but any Christian man who is a baptized member of the Brethren may choose a hymn, pray, or say whatever he feels God wants him to say during the time of worship. A single cup of wine is passed from person to person.

5 Prayer is about Real Life!
Have you watched the news recently? Try drawing a flowchart of the news. Opposite is an example to help you.

Now look carefully at the Intercessions from the Alternative Service Book (see the box). Copy and complete the flowchart of the Intercessions, using items from the news to help you fill in the boxes.

6 For discussion
How might the Peace help Christians to feel that they were all part of the same worldwide Christian family?

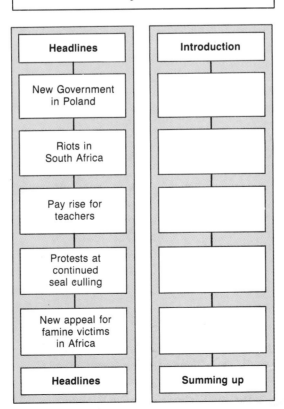

Intercessions

Let us pray for the Church and for the world, and let us thank God for his goodness.

Almighty God, our heavenly Father, you promised through your Son Jesus Christ to hear us when we pray in faith.

Strengthen *N* our bishop and all your Church in the service of Christ; that those who confess your name may be united in your truth, live together in your love, and reveal
           your glory in the world.

Give grace to us, our families and friends, and to all our neighbours; that we may serve Christ in one another, and love as he loves us.

Comfort and heal all those who suffer in body, mind, or spirit . . .; give them courage and hope in their troubles; and bring them
           the joy of your salvation.

Lord, in your mercy
hear our prayer.

Alternative Service Book

THE JOB OF THE CHRISTIAN

Jesus left his followers with a job to do. It involved telling other people about God as well as doing the work, which Jesus himself began, of helping other · people. Christians now have the same responsibilities.

Attending church services is only part of what worshipping God really means. Real worship involves seeing other people as God sees them, and trying to put the teaching of Jesus into practice.

ORGANIZATION

For some people, this will mean being involved with the organization of the church. Each local church has a group of people who help to organize the work of that church. Sometimes they are called **deacons**, sometimes the **church council**. This group of people share in the responsibility of organizing each local group of Christians in their task of serving God. They recognize that serving God often means serving other people. The 'other people' may be somewhere on the other side of the world, or part of the local community.

A Responsibilities in God's family

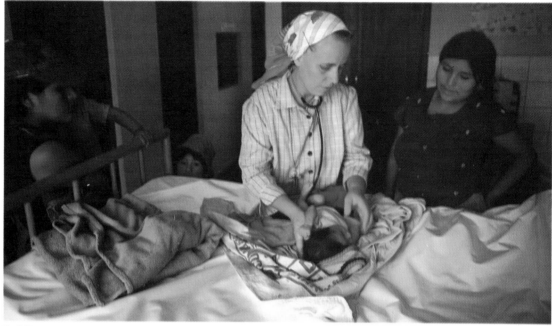

B Mission clinic, Bolivia

ALL PART OF WORSHIP

a Responsibilities to the local community

Many churches have a variety of ways in which they try to help the local community. These include Old People's clubs, Playgroups, Mother and Toddler groups, Women's groups, as well as Youth groups, Scouts, Guides, and often many others. These are often regarded as a way of showing God's love in the world, by trying to help people to get to know one another, and to care about one another. When people get too old or ill to attend church services or the Old People's club, then the church will try to show that they continue to care, by going on visiting. This will often involve the priest taking Communion to the old or sick people so that they can continue to feel that they are part of the worshipping community.

Many churches like to arrange to visit members and other people from their area when they are in hospital. One of the ways in which young people can begin to accept responsibility in the church is by becoming involved in visiting old people and others who find it impossible to get about.

b Elsewhere in the world

Some Christians are involved with mission partners, who are people who feel that God has told them to spend part of their lives in another country, or environment, helping people there to work out what God wants them to do with their lives. Sometimes this will mean being directly involved in telling other people about Jesus. It may also involve doing a very necessary job alongside local people. For example, missionary societies often send agricultural experts or medical experts to areas of the world where their skills can particularly help local people towards a better quality of life.

Churches in the developed world try to help provide money to continue to show God's love for the world in this particular way. Some Christians take on the responsibilities of keeping in touch with mission partners, who often have to lead a very lonely life, and very much appreciate news from home.

C 'Sing to the Lord a new song'

c Within the local church

Many Christians help with the organization of the local church itself. There are certain administrative jobs. These include secretarial tasks, as well as looking after the money which Christians contribute towards the work which each church does. Those with musical talents may find that they become involved in the musical side of worship. Others may find their way of serving God is by being a server, or helping teach others about Jesus. A few people will discover that their job is to serve God in a special way, by becoming a priest or minister, or a

mission partner, or some other kind of full time Christian work.

Every Christian has the responsibility of using the gifts and abilities which they believe God has given to them. It is the church's job to help each individual discover what their own gifts are, and to help them to develop that gift, in the service of God and of other people.

NOTES/DATABASE

Look up the following words in the glossary. Then use the definitions to make suitable entries for your notebook or database.

Deacons   Church Council

The Choristers' Prayer

Bless O Lord
Us thy servants
Who minister in thy temple.
Grant that what we sing with our lips
We may believe in our hearts,
And what we believe in our hearts
We may show forth in our lives.
Through Jesus Christ our Lord.
Amen.

ACTIVITIES

1 **Quick quiz**

a What job did Jesus tell his followers to do?

b What are some of the names given to the groups which organize church life?

c Why do you think that Christians try to serve God through serving other people?

d Make a list of some of the ways in which churches try to help the local community.

e How does the church try to help old or ill people to feel that they are still a part of the worshipping community?

f What is one way in which Christian young people can begin to accept the responsibility of being a Christian?

g What are mission partners?

h Make a list of some of the activities in which mission partners can be involved.

i How can churches at home help mission partners?

j In what ways do you think that mission partners might find the life they lead difficult?

k What kind of jobs need doing in the organization of the local church?

l Make a list of the special ways in which some people may feel that they want to serve God.

m Is there any member of the Christian Church who does not have a job to do? Write down some reasons for your answer.

D Preparing for a service

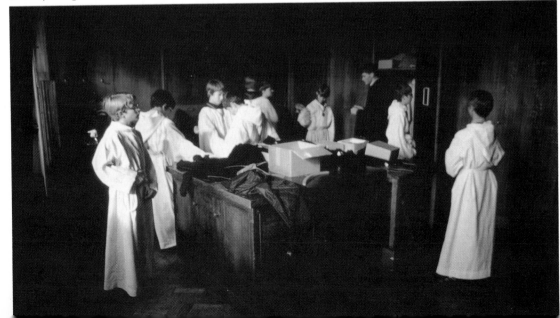

FURTHER ACTIVITIES

SITUATIONS VACANT

Servers needed
Male or female. Age 12 or over. Must be reliable. No previous experience necessary. Training given.

Church Council
Nominations are invited for the Church Council. Each nominee should be proposed and seconded, and proposers should check that nominees are willing to stand for elections.

Help Needed!
Help is needed at the Mother and Toddler club every Tuesday afternoon. If you feel you could look after children, make tea, chat to mums, wash up or sweep up, you are probably the person we are looking for!

Bible study
The topic for the next six weeks will be 'Put on the whole armour of God' (Ephesians 6:10). Open to anyone. We all learn by listening to one another. Bring a Bible and try to read this section through first. Wednesday evening at Ian's house.

Prayer meeting
Any new members who would like to meet to take on the job of praying for our church and the church throughout the world, please contact Sarah.

Vacancies exist for choristers
Boys and girls over the age of 8 may audition as sopranos. Altos, tenors and basses also needed. Two services per Sunday, plus festivals. Large number of weddings for which there is a small payment.

Organist urgently needed
Excellent pipe organ, full choir, two services per Sunday. Payment by arrangement.

Parish Secretary Required
To help busy vicar. Mornings only.

Keep in touch scheme
If you would like to keep in touch with our link missionaries in Port Said, please contact Elizabeth who organizes the writing of regular letters.

Annual Christian Aid collection
Collectors needed for several more streets. If you feel you can help, please contact John Hughes.

1 Jobs Galore!

a Which of the jobs shown on the left would be open to any member of the church?

b Why do you think that being members of prayer meeting and Bible study groups are shown as being jobs within the church?

c Which jobs might you need special skills for?

d Do you think that there would be any Christian who was left without a part to play in the church? Write down some reasons for your answer.

2 Design your own 'Situations Vacant' board
There are many other jobs in a church which have not been included in the advertisements shown here. See how many you can write advertisements for. (Don't forget the cleaning, the heating, and the grounds etc.)

THE THINGS SOME PEOPLE DO

After I was baptized (when I was 15), I decided to try to give back something to the church instead of being on the receiving end all the time. I decided to ask the minister what he thought I could help with, and he suggested, of all things, that I might like to help deliver the church magazine. I thought this was an awful job and I didn't really want to do it, but I decided to give it a try. I soon found that some of the people on my round were old people who scarcely saw anyone all week, and were really very lonely. So when one of them offered me a cup of tea, I accepted. Soon I was visiting several of these people, even when I didn't have to deliver the church magazine, and I felt that I was really beginning to do what God wanted me to do.

Matthew Aged 15

When the vicar asked me to help with 'Lamplighters' (our kids' club on a Monday evening), I was quite horrified. I was scared stiff at the idea of teaching these children about the Bible and playing daft games with them. Even worse were the songs they sang. At first I felt really embarrassed, but now I wouldn't miss it for anything. The kids are great fun, and I really miss the club when I can't turn up. I'm meant to be helping, but I've learned so much from the kids. They have helped me to understand more about what worshipping God really means.

Jane, aged 14

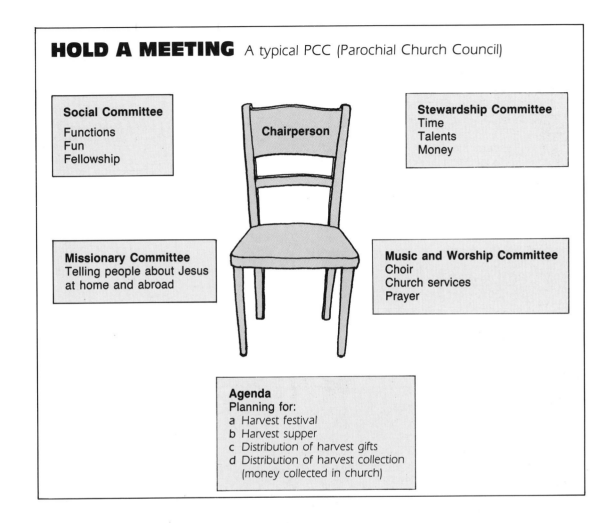

HOLD A MEETING A typical PCC (Parochial Church Council)

Social Committee
Functions
Fun
Fellowship

Chairperson

Stewardship Committee
Time
Talents
Money

Missionary Committee
Telling people about Jesus
at home and abroad

Music and Worship Committee
Choir
Church services
Prayer

Agenda
Planning for:
a Harvest festival
b Harvest supper
c Distribution of harvest gifts
d Distribution of harvest collection
(money collected in church)

Name	Matthew	Jane
Job		
a What has been learnt		
b ...		

3 **Read what Matthew and Jane do in their churches**

a What jobs do Matthew and Jane do in their churches?

b What qualities do you think they each need for the jobs they do?

c Copy the chart on the right and fill it in with the things which you think they have each learnt through doing these jobs.

4 **Now answer these questions**

a Match the correct agenda item to each of the sub-committees of the PCC.

b Split up into groups, each discussing one agenda item as though you were the appropriate sub-committee (e.g. the correct committee should plan the harvest service and return with a service plan).

c Make a written report, as well as a spoken one, which includes the plan worked out by your committee for that part of the harvest celebrations.

CHOOSING A CAREER

As young people grow up, they begin to think about the way in which they will spend their adult lives. For most, this will mean a job of some kind. At school they will have begun to investigate some of the career options open to them. They will be helped to think about the kind of things which they are good at, which they enjoy doing, and perhaps to see how these can begin to fit in with a career.

A Choosing a career

CHRISTIAN BELIEF AFFECTS DECISIONS

Christian young people wish to be sure that their career fits in with God's plan for their lives. Most churches will encourage young people to think about what they want to do with their lives, and also to pray about it.

This does not mean that they will be encouraged to do 'holy' jobs. Christians believe that most people should serve God in their everyday situations, doing ordinary jobs. Many people find their Christian **vocation** in their work – in shops, or offices, or factories.

VOLUNTARY SERVICE OVERSEAS

Some young people decide to spend time working for other people before embarking on their career. Joining Voluntary Service Overseas, a secular organization, is one way in which they can do this. Volunteers work for a year in various situations, such as teaching in Developing World countries, or perhaps acting as agricultural consultants in an area where farming is difficult. Very often, this kind of experience helps those volunteers who are Christians to work out the way in which they believe God wants them to spend the rest of their lives.

> **vocation** . . . a job which one does because one thinks one has a special fitness or ability to give service to other people . . .
> . . . a special calling from, or choosing by, God for the religious life . . .
> *Longman's Dictionary*

B Voluntary Service Overseas

Many Christians like to extend the meaning of vocation to every kind of job. They believe they are serving God in whatever job they do.

SPECIAL WAYS OF SERVING GOD

There are some people, of course, who believe that the way God wants them to serve him is by being a minister or priest, or sometimes by living as a member of a religious community.

ORDINATION

The usual word for becoming a minister or priest is **ordination**. In the Eastern Orthodox and Roman Catholic churches, only men are ordained. The Anglican Church in a number of countries allows women to be ordained, and most of the Free Churches allow women to be admitted to the ministry.

C 'Take authority' . . .

APPROPRIATE PEOPLE

Young people who decide that they wish to serve God in this particular way have a fairly long and difficult training ahead of them. The Church, too, wishes to make sure that it is choosing the appropriate people for the job of ministry. It carries immense responsibilities in terms of helping other people to feel that they are in the right relationship with God, and in leading worship. Ministers and priests are often privileged to know the intimate details of many people's lives and to be with people at moments of great sadness as well as great joy. The Church, therefore, has a fairly rigorous selection procedure even before someone can begin training for the **ministry**.

After several years of training, there is a service in which the new minister or priest is commissioned by the church for the job they will do in the future. In many churches this ceremony is called ordination. The newly ordained person receives the authority to work in the church and in the world. It is also an opportunity for individuals to worship God and to offer their lives and work to God and to other people.

NOTES/DATABASE

Look up the following words in the glossary. Then use the definitions to make suitable entries for your notebook or database.

Ministry   Ordination   Vocation

D 'Take authority' . . . a Kenyan priest

ACTIVITIES

1 **Quick quiz**

a Make a list of the factors which you consider important in choosing a career.

b What other factor will Christian young people wish to consider?

c What will churches encourage Christian young people to do as part of their career decisions?

d In which kind of job do Christians believe that most people serve God?

e What is one way in which young people can help other people for a year or so before embarking on a career?

f How do you think this kind of experience might help in career choice?

g What does the word 'vocation' mean?

h How do many Christians extend the meaning of the word 'vocation'?

i What does the word 'ordination' mean?

j In which churches are women as well as men allowed to become ministers?

k Why does the church need to make sure that the appropriate people are chosen to be ministers and priests?

l Why do you think that the Church insists upon several years of training for the ministry?

m What does the ceremony of ordination provide the opportunity for the individual to do?

1 Class survey

Carry out a survey to find out what members of your class think is important when choosing a career.

Design your survey form carefully so that it is easy to fill in. If you have access to a computer, use a word processor and desk top publishing system to design and print your survey form. Here is a suggestion to help you.

Deciding on a career

SURVEY FORM

a Have you decided on a career yet?
Yes ☐ No ☐

b If yes, what career are you considering?

[   ]

c Would you like to work with people?
Yes ☐ No ☐

d Do you enjoy making things?
Yes ☐ No ☐

e Do you enjoy practical subjects?
Yes ☐ No ☐

f Are you expecting to go on to higher education?
Yes ☐ No ☐

g What are you good at at school?

[   ]

h Which school subjects have influenced your career choice?

[   ]

i Have your parents influenced your choice of career?
Yes ☐ No ☐

FURTHER ACTIVITIES

2 Use your results

When you have collected all the results of the survey, make a chart of the results.

Now change your questions so that they would be appropriate to adults who are already in a job. Add an extra question:

On a scale of 1–10, how important is it to do the job which you think God wants you to do?

3 Now answer these questions

a Why do you think that the Anglican Church makes a deacon serve a year before becoming a priest?

b Do you think it right that 23 years is the minimum age for ordination as a priest in the Anglican Church?

c Is 30 too young to be a bishop? Give reasons for your answer.

d Do you think that anyone who wishes to be ordained ought to do an ordinary job for some time first? Give reasons for your answer. Make a list of what you think would be suitable jobs.

ORDINATION

In many ways an ordination is similar to a confirmation. In the Eastern Orthodox, Roman Catholic and Anglican churches, the candidate, usually called the ordinand, kneels in front of the bishop. He puts his hands on the candidate's head. He prays for a special gift of the Holy Spirit which will enable that person to do the job of a minister.

There are three 'orders' of ministry in these churches

E Deacons

F Priest

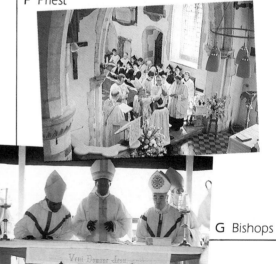

G Bishops

WOMEN IN THE MINISTRY

Recently, there has been a great deal of discussion about women being ordained.

The argument against women priests

The argument against women priests centres around Paul's instructions in the Bible that women should keep silent in church. Some Christians also argue that Jesus' disciples were all men, and that Jesus himself was a man, therefore there should be no women priests.

The argument in favour of women priests

The argument for women priests recognizes that there were many women among Jesus' followers even though they are not named as the special twelve. There are also women in the New Testament who are mentioned as leaders in the church, and deaconesses are mentioned in the New Testament. Paul also says that by believing in Jesus, everyone is equal.

'There is no difference between slave or free, male or female, Jew or Greek' (Galatians 3:28).

NO PRIESTS AT ALL!

The Christian Brethren, and some other Christian groups, believe that it is wrong to have paid, full time ministers at all. They argue that the disciples were ordinary people who had ordinary jobs and were not trained in the very specialized way that clergy are trained now. St Paul, they argue, was a tentmaker and earned his living sewing tents. He was proud to go around the world telling people about Jesus and being able to earn his living at the same time. They also say that 1 Corinthians 12 and other passages in the Bible show that the church is made up of ordinary people. These people have lots of gifts which can be used in the service of Christ, and it is right to use everyone's gifts. They suggest that ordination sets someone apart in a way which is contrary to Scripture.

The Bible emphasizes that Christians are brothers and sisters because they believe in Jesus. Although they have leaders at their services, any Christian man has the right to say whatever he feels God wants him to say during one of their services of Breaking of Bread. A very similar attitude is held by Quakers, although their worship does not include a form of Eucharist.

4 Over to you!

Imagine you are taking part in a phone-in show. Phone in and state your views. You will need to appoint a chairperson to listen carefully and sum up everyone's opinions.

What do you think about the ordination of women?

Should this, like other jobs, be open to women?

Should people be able to choose whether they go to a woman or a man to receive Holy Communion?

Would you like your marriage to be carried out by a woman?

Now that you have heard other people's views, write about the following subject:

Should women be priests?

5 For discussion

Do you think it is right to have a paid, full time ministry? Or do you think it is better to have people willing to do the work of the Church whilst remaining in ordinary jobs?

RELIGIOUS COMMUNITIES

Throughout history, there have been some people who have made a decision not to get married. Sometimes this has been for religious reasons. Within the Roman Catholic and Eastern Orthodox churches there are still many people who choose to spend their lives in religious communities. They sometimes serve God through a life of prayer. Many religious communities are involved in social work or teaching. One example of a modern religious community whose lives are dedicated to helping the poorest of the poor is the Sisters of Mercy, an Order of nuns, founded in Calcutta by Mother Teresa. Another example is the Jesuit Order of monks who have been dedicated to teaching since the 16th century. These two groups are **celibate** Orders. Their members have decided that they can serve God better by not getting

B A life of prayer

A Dedicated to teaching

married. They have promised that they will have no money, never marry, and will always be obedient to their religious superiors. This way of serving God is the vocation of comparatively few Christians.

MODERN COMMUNITIES

In the 20th century, religious communities have been formed which consist of both single and married people. An example of one of these is the Community of the Celebration. This is an Anglican community which also welcomes people from other **denominations**.

The Community of the Celebration is very active in helping churches worship God in a way which is exciting and full of joy. Communities such as this are one way in which today's Christians have tried to work for God. They include married and single people from all walks of life, both rich and poor alike.

C Work at Buckfast Abbey

MARRIAGE

When Christian people decide to get married they will have considered some of the same kinds of questions that they considered when thinking of a career. 'Is this the person with whom I wish to spend the rest of my life?' is one question. The second – 'Is this what God wants for us both?' – is just as important to Christians.

Christians usually choose to be married in church. Very often the bride chooses to wear white, which is a traditional colour for weddings and symbolizes purity. In both a register office wedding and a Christian marriage in church, the couple make promises of their intention to live together for life, to the exclusion of all others. These promises are made to each other in the presence of a person with the legal authority to marry them, such as a **registrar** or **clergyman**.

In Christian marriage, the promises are made to each other in the presence of God. The couple ask for God's help in keeping their vows to each other. Prayers are said for the couple to ask God's blessing as they begin their married life together. The couple usually invite their families and friends to the wedding. Marriages are traditionally a time for family reunions and there is often a wedding reception after the service.

DIFFICULTIES

Although Christians recognize that a large percentage of marriages end in divorce, marriage promises are made for life. No Christians ever set out on a marriage thinking that if it doesn't work out, they can get a divorce. The Roman Catholic Church only recognizes divorces in rare cases.

In recent years, where marriages do break down, churches have taken a more loving and forgiving view. Many of them have counselling services to help in difficulties and are frequently prepared to allow divorced people to remarry in church.

NOTES/DATABASE

Look up the following words in the glossary. Then use the definitions to construct suitable entries for your notebook or database.

Celibate	Denomination
Registrar	Clergyman

ACTIVITIES

1 **Quick quiz**

a Write down *one* religious reason why people have sometimes decided to remain single.

b Name *two* types of work in which religious communities are sometimes involved.

c Which modern community was founded in Calcutta?

d What is the aim of this community?

e What type of work is done by the Jesuits?

f What does the word 'celibate' mean?

g What *three* promises do members of celibate orders make?

h What kind of people are members of the Community of the Celebration?

i What questions do Christians ask themselves when they are thinking about getting married?

j In a church wedding in Britain, why does the bride often choose to wear white?

k To whom are the promises made in a Christian wedding?

l Why do you think weddings are often a time for family reunions?

m How can churches show a loving attitude when marriages break down?

CHRISTIAN MARRIAGE

In every society, there have always been special ceremonies attached to the time when a man and a woman decide that they want to commit themselves to one another for the rest of their lives, and to have children together. It has been the Christian custom for a person to have only one partner. Within Christianity, men and women are equal in status though they may have different functions within society. Their different function should never mean that one is in any way better than the other. One way of expressing this equality is by monogamy, or having only one partner.

D 'With this ring I thee wed'

FURTHER ACTIVITIES

Christian marriage is an equal partnership, calling for total commitment on the part of each partner. Ideally, it exists to provide close companionship for two people in all circumstances, as well as a safe and happy environment for children.

Look carefully at these promises made during a marriage service:

The priest receives the ring(s). He says

Heavenly Father, by your blessing, let *this ring* be to *N* and *N* a symbol of unending love and faithfulness, to remind them of the vow and covenant which they have made this day; through Jesus Christ our Lord. **Amen.**

The bridegroom places the ring on the fourth finger of the bride's left hand, and holding it there, says

I give you this ring
as a sign of our marriage.
With my body I honour you,
all that I am I give to you,
and all that I have I share with you,
within the love of God,
Father, Son, and Holy Spirit.

If only one ring is used, before they loose hands the bride says

I receive this ring
as a sign of our marriage.
With my body I honour you,
all that I am I give to you,
and all that I have I share with you,
within the love of God,
Father, Son, and Holy Spirit.

Alternative Service Book, 1980

---

1 Who is important?
One of the best known weddings that ever happened is the marriage at Cana in John 2:1ff, and we don't even know the bride's name. In fact, all we really know about is what happened at the reception.

Read through the story then discuss these points.

a What reasons can you think of for this story often being used as a Bible reading at a marriage service?

b Read through Paul's advice about marriage in I Corinthians 7:1–5. Make a list of the advice which Paul gives.

---

2 Now answer these questions

a What do you think is the most important part of marriage?

b Why do you think it has often been considered important to have a ceremony in which the marriage partners make their promises before God as well as to one another?

c Do you think it would help two people during times of difficulty to know that their promises involved God as well as one another?

d In your own words, write down what you think the marriage promises mean.

THE SIX PARTS OF CHRISTIAN MARRIAGE

1. What is marriage for?

2. Can they be legally married?

3. Do they <u>want</u> to be married?

4. a) Bride's father gives her to the groom.

   b) The giving and receiving of a ring.

5. Legal statement that they are now married.

6. Prayers for God's help in their marriage.

3 Plan a service

Many churches have marriage service books or leaflets. Try to borrow some of these from several different denominations.

a Find out what is similar and what is different in each church. Compare the service in the book you have with the flowchart of a marriage service on this page.

b Choose one of the services and plan your ideal wedding, including prayers, readings from the Bible, and suitable hymns.

WHAT THE BIBLE SAYS ABOUT MARRIAGE

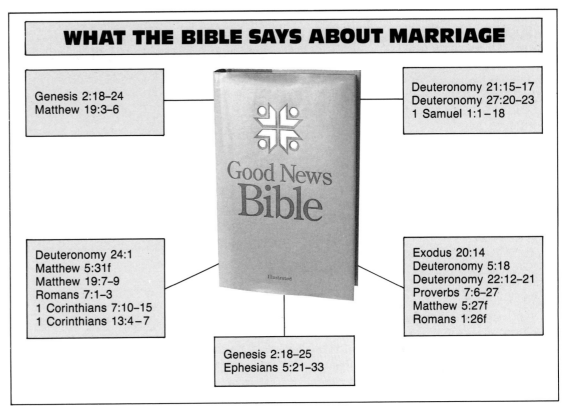

Genesis 2:18–24
Matthew 19:3–6

Deuteronomy 21:15–17
Deuteronomy 27:20–23
1 Samuel 1:1–18

Deuteronomy 24:1
Matthew 5:31f
Matthew 19:7–9
Romans 7:1–3
1 Corinthians 7:10–15
1 Corinthians 13:4–7

Exodus 20:14
Deuteronomy 5:18
Deuteronomy 22:12–21
Proverbs 7:6–27
Matthew 5:27f
Romans 1:26f

Genesis 2:18–25
Ephesians 5:21–33

4 Look up these Bible references
Copy and complete the chart.
Enter the appropriate verse in the correct column.

Two people become one	
One wife only	
Sex only within marriage	
Different roles for husband and wife	
Marriages should be permanent	

CHRISTIAN FAITH INCLUDES RESPECT FOR THE ELDERLY

Respect and care for older people has been part of the Christian message from the start. In the Old Testament, the Ten Commandments taught the people of Israel:

Honour your father and your mother, so that your own days may be long in the land which the Lord your God gives you.
Exodus 20:12

In other words, parents need to set the example to their children by looking after their relatives so that when they are old, their children will take care of them, and so on.

Again, in the New Testament, care for the widows in the Christian community was part of being a Christian. True worship of God is always impossible without a caring attitude towards other people.

A 'Honour your father and your mother'

B A new purpose in life

NEW PURPOSE IN LIFE FOR RETIRED PEOPLE

The Church today continues to respect older people's experience of life. Many elderly people continue to serve God in a very active way long into old age. Numerous retired people find a new purpose in life in **voluntary work**, sometimes within a church. They are freer to help others in ways which are not open to those with commitments to jobs and families. Many older people do very valuable work in helping others, often much younger than themselves. On a practical level, this can sometimes take the form of providing transport to hospital etc, for mothers with young children, or perhaps listening to those people who need someone to talk to about their problems.

THE CHURCH'S CARE FOR THE ELDERLY

The Church has always organized clubs and social events for elderly people, as well as providing worship services at times which are convenient to them. These clubs provide **fellowship**, one of the essentials of Christian life. Usually they are very active, cheerful places,

where the members are conscious when any of their number become too old or frail to join in the activities any longer. Members will take on the task of visiting these people, helping them to feel that they still belong to the group. The minister will usually visit them fairly frequently, either to pray with them or to take Communion to them. In this way, elderly people are able to feel that they are still part of the worshipping family of God. Many churches also have 'prayer chains', or groups of people who pray for individuals and the work of the whole church. Many house-bound people like to take part in this. Christians believe that prayer changes things and people, and being involved in prayer helps elderly people to feel that they are continuing to play a useful part in church life.

C Still part of the family of God

GOD IS STILL IN CHARGE

Eventually, death must come to all of us. Many of us are frightened by death because it remains, for everyone, a mystery. Christians believe that their religion is about death as well as about life. They believe that Christianity is a preparation for death as well as a way in which life may be lived to the full. When death does come, it is not the end. Even though death may still be a time of great sadness, and sometimes of pain, Christians believe that the death of Jesus Christ, on the Cross, brought about a victory over death. According to Christians, those who die, believing in Jesus, will have a new kind of life, called 'Eternal Life'. This is known as belief in the **Resurrection**. Each time Christians say the Creed (a statement of Christian belief) they say,

D Christian funeral

'We believe . . .
in the Resurrection of the dead, and the life of the world to come.

BURIAL SERVICES

This Christian hope is expressed in Christian burial services. These are very simple services in which the body of the person who has died is committed to God. The body is either buried in the ground or burned at a crematorium. Prayers, Bible readings and Psalms all remind the bereaved people (the friends and relations of the dead person) of the Christian belief in the Resurrection. There are hymns expressing the Christian faith. The minister may give a short talk about the dead person to say what they were like when they were alive, with a summary of some of the things they accomplished during their life.

Christians believe that God is in charge of all that happens, including death. They live their lives knowing that, even in death, God will not let them down.

NOTES/DATABASE

Look up the following words in the glossary. Then use the definitions to make suitable entries for your notebook or database.

Fellowship   Resurrection

Voluntary work

ACTIVITIES

1 **Quick quiz**
   a What do the Ten Commandments teach about care for elderly people?

   b What kinds of things do retired people do to help in the church family?

   c Why do you think their help is so useful?

   d In what ways does the Church try to help elderly people?

   e How can Christians help someone, who is too old or frail to go out, to feel that they are still a part of the worshipping family of God?

   f How could being a member of a prayer chain help someone to feel that they still had a useful part to play in the Church?

   g Write down *one* thing which Christians believe about prayer.

   h Write down *one* thing which Christians believe about death.

   i What do Christians say about the Resurrection in the Creed?

   j Make a list of the parts of a burial service which help the bereaved people to understand more about the Christian belief in the Resurrection.

   k How do you think it might help Christians to believe that, throughout their lives, God is in charge?

RESPECT OLD PEOPLE

The Bible takes it for granted that old people will be cared for within the family. There are laws to make sure that widows, for example, are properly looked after. Respect for the elderly is emphasized, and there are guidelines laid down for this.

2 Look up the following verses about respect for older people
It may help you if you make a note of what each of these verses says.
Exodus 20:12
Exodus 21:17
Leviticus 19:32
Mark 7:9–12
1 Timothy 5:4,8

3 Now write a magazine article
Call it 'Respect for the elderly, a Biblical viewpoint'. Use the references quoted above to help you work out what you think the Bible teaches about respecting old people.

GROWING OLDER IN GOD'S FAMILY

FURTHER ACTIVITIES

1 Who cares?

Here are some organizations which work with old people. Choose one of these, and write to them for some information about their work.

a Age Concern

Bernard Sunley House
Pitcairn Road
Mitcham
Surrey CR4 3LL

This coordinates local efforts to help old people all over Britain.

b The National Corporation for the Care of Old People

Nuffield Lodge
Regents Park
London NW1 4RS

Set up in 1947, this researches ways in which money can best be used to help old people.

c The Salvation Army

Schools Information Service,
101 Queen Victoria Street,
London EC4P 4EP

An international religious organization founded in 1865 which helps to care for young and old people, the sick and the homeless. The Salvation Army provides project packs free of charge for schools.

d Help the Aged

1 St James Walk
London EC1R 0BE

A Christian-based international charity, set up in 1962, helping old people worldwide, and especially during famines, natural disasters etc. Money is channelled through relief teams, churches, Red Cross etc. Help the Aged provides literature for schools and also publishes a newspaper.

2 An advertising campaign

When you have received the information, use it to plan an advertising campaign within your school to tell more young people about the work of that charity. You will need to design posters, and ask for permission to put them up in appropriate spots. Decide which spots in your school create the biggest impact. Tape a two-minute appeal for help, giving information which will make other people wish to help in working to help old people.

Use a word processor and desk top publishing package for this activity if you have access to a computer.

BELIEF IN THE RESURRECTION

Jesus said, 'I am the resurrection and the life.'

3 Read carefully John 11:1–44

a Why do you think that Jesus delayed two more days after he heard that Lazarus was ill?

b How do you think the disciples felt when they discovered that Lazarus was already dead?

c What did Martha say to Jesus? (verse 21)

d Explain clearly what happened after Jesus was taken to see the tomb. Use verses 38–44 to help you.

4 For discussion

How do you think the raising of Lazarus might help a Christian to understand more about the Resurrection of Jesus?

Extra food for thought

Paul's teaching about the Resurrection is in 1 Corinthians 15:12–58. It is in difficult language, with complex ideas. Some of you may like to read this to gain an extra insight into the Christian belief in the Resurrection.

The Burial Service
Committal
The minister says:
EITHER
For as much as *our brother* has departed out of this life, and Almighty God in his great mercy has called *him* to himself, we therefore commit *his* body to the ground, earth to earth, ashes to ashes, dust to dust, in sure and certain hope of the resurrection to eternal life through our Lord Jesus Christ, to whom be glory for ever.
Amen.
OR
For as much as *our brother* has departed out of this life, we therefore commit *his* body to the ground, earth to earth, ashes to ashes, dust to dust, trusting in the infinite mercy of God, in Jesus Christ our Lord. **Amen**

Alternative Service Book

5 Now answer these questions

a Which phrases are different in the alternative forms of the committal given on the left hand page?

b Which version states the Christian belief in the Resurrection more clearly? Write down some reasons for your answer.

c If someone had been a committed Christian all their life, which version do you think that their bereaved relations might prefer? Give reasons for suggesting this.

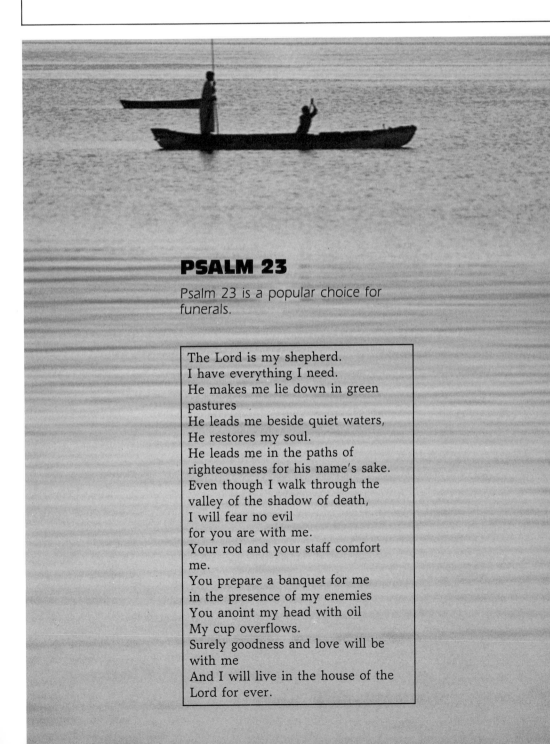

PSALM 23

Psalm 23 is a popular choice for funerals.

The Lord is my shepherd.
I have everything I need.
He makes me lie down in green pastures
He leads me beside quiet waters,
He restores my soul.
He leads me in the paths of righteousness for his name's sake.
Even though I walk through the valley of the shadow of death,
I will fear no evil
for you are with me.
Your rod and your staff comfort me.
You prepare a banquet for me
in the presence of my enemies
You anoint my head with oil
My cup overflows.
Surely goodness and love will be with me
And I will live in the house of the Lord for ever.

6 Read Psalm 23

a Why do you think this Psalm is often chosen at funerals?

b In what ways do you think this Psalm might be helpful to someone who was very ill?

c This Psalm expresses the Christian belief that God is in control of the life of the believer. Do you think it might help a Christian who was suffering pain to believe this? Write down some reasons for your answer.

A TIME OF HOPE

Christians believe that after they die, they will rise again to spend eternity with God. So for Christians, although funerals may be sad for the relatives and people who attend, they can also be occasions full of joy because the person who has died has gone to be with God.

7 For discussion

a In what variety of ways have you seen people react when someone has died?

b Is it possible for an event to be both sad, and also a time for joy? Give reasons.

THE LIFE OF JESUS IS AT THE CENTRE

The Church's year revolves around the story of the life of Christ. Each year Christians hear, Sunday by Sunday, the events of the life of Jesus on which their faith is based.

Christianity is an historical religion. Almost everything which Christians celebrate has an historical event behind it.

LECTIONARIES

The older churches, that is the Eastern Orthodox, the Roman Catholic and the Anglican churches, have a set pattern of readings from the Bible, Psalms and prayers. These form the basis of the teaching and worship in church each Sunday. The clergy in these churches are also expected to say services, including their own prayers and Bible readings each day, there is a daily pattern as well. This is called the **lectionary**. Throughout the year, the Sunday readings are specially planned to take Christians through the life of Jesus. There are also readings from the Old Testament and the New Testament letters which are linked carefully to the main reading, or **Gospel**. The Gospel is always taken from Matthew, Mark, Luke or John. These four books are called Gospels, and it is from them that we get most of our information about the events of the life of Jesus.

FLEXIBILITY

Other Christian churches celebrate the major festivals of Christianity but, in their services, the minister or preacher is free to adopt whatever readings he or she wishes to fit in with the teaching they have prepared. The prayers are also at the discretion of the person leading them and are not usually written down. Instead the leader will pray about whatever he or she believes God wants the Christians in that place to pray about. This is called **extempore prayer**.

A Festival decorations

Many Christians follow patterns of Bible readings, contained in helpful daily notes about the Bible. These are useful in helping people organize their Bible reading so that they read all parts of the Bible, not just the familiar parts.

MAJOR CHRISTIAN FESTIVALS

The major Christian festivals are times of great joy. The three great festivals, celebrated throughout the Christian world, are Christmas, which remembers the birth of Jesus; Easter, in which his death and resurrection are celebrated; and Pentecost, when the disciples were given the gift of the Holy Spirit. This gave them the power to tell the world about Jesus.

PREPARATION FOR FESTIVALS

Each of these festivals has a period of preparation leading up to it. Before Christmas comes the season of Advent. Christians focus their attention on the prophecies about the birth of a special messenger from God. He was to be called the **Messiah** or anointed one. His job was to put God's wishes right into the hearts of people so that they would do what God wanted them to do. Christians believe that Jesus was this special person. During Advent, Christians also hear about John the Baptist, whose job it was to announce the coming of the Messiah.

The season of preparation for Easter is called Lent. During Lent Christians remember that Jesus spent 40 days and 40 nights without food in the desert. Lent also lasts 40 days.

After Easter, there is a period of preparation for the gift of the Holy Spirit at Pentecost. During this time, Christians are encouraged to think about the resurrection appearances. For a period of six weeks, after he had died and risen from the dead, Jesus was with his disciples, teaching them and preparing them for their job of telling the world about him. The time between Easter and Pentecost is therefore six weeks.

TELLING THE WORLD ABOUT JESUS

When the disciples received the gift of the Holy Spirit at Pentecost, it was given to them so that they could tell the world about Jesus. After Pentecost, in the

Church's year, comes a section of the year in which Christians remember how the disciples did this. It is also an encouragement for Christians to put into practice Jesus' instructions:

'Go into all the world, and make disciples of all nations baptizing people everywhere in the name of the Father, the Son and the Holy Spirit.'

(Matthew 28:19)

B Festival banner

C Stained glass by Chagal

NOTES/DATABASE

Look up the following words in the glossary. Then use the definitions to make suitable entries for your notebook or database.

Gospel	Gospels
Extempore prayer	Messiah
Lectionary	

ACTIVITIES

1 **Quick quiz**

a On what events is the Christian calendar based?

b Make a list of Christian festivals which are based on historical events.

c Which churches follow a set pattern of Bible readings and prayers?

d How do the other churches decide which Bible readings they will use?

e From which books of the Bible do we get most of our information about the life of Jesus?

f What is extempore prayer?

g How do many Christians organize their own bible readings?

h What do Christians celebrate at Christmas?

i What is celebrated at Easter?

j What gift did the disciples receive at Pentecost?

k Why do you think that the Church has a time of preparation before each of the great festivals?

l Name *two* of the seasons of preparation.

m What was the gift of the Holy Spirit for?

n Which of Jesus' instructions are Christians encouraged to put into practice after they have learned about the gift of the Holy Spirit at Pentecost?

FURTHER ACTIVITIES

1 Look up each Bible reference in the diagram of the Church's year
This will tell you which part of the life of Jesus is celebrated during the season marked at the top of the box.

Now copy the flowchart of the life of Jesus and the birth of the church, and enter the correct seasons in the empty boxes connected to each of the sections of the life of Jesus.

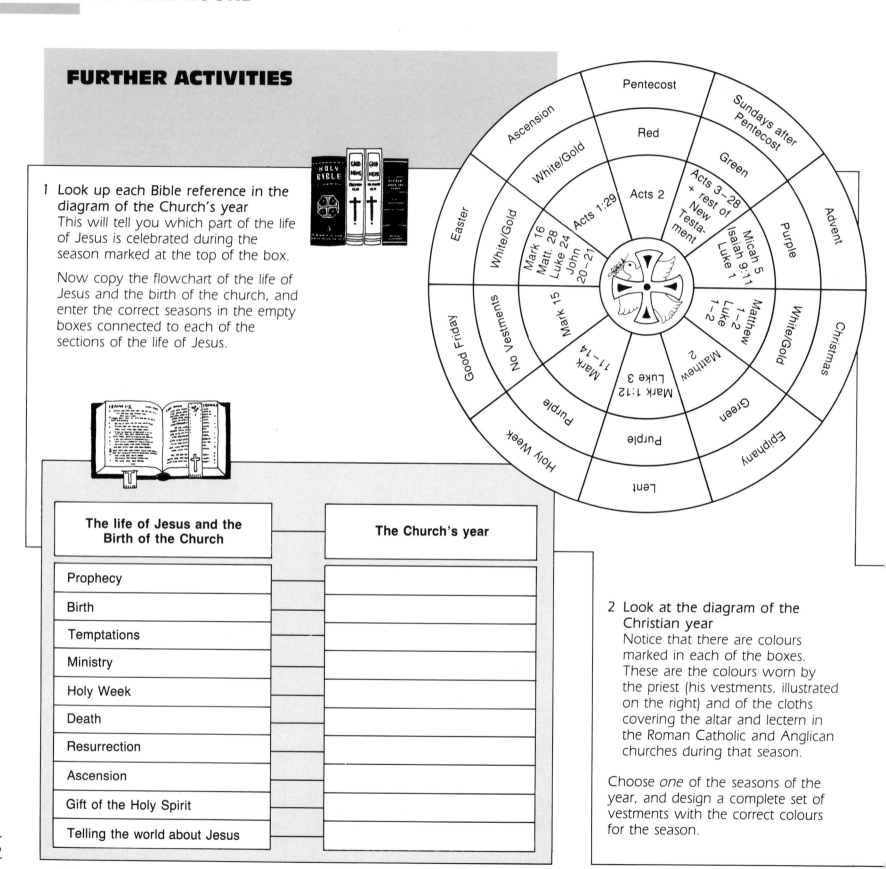

The life of Jesus and the Birth of the Church		The Church's year
Prophecy		
Birth		
Temptations		
Ministry		
Holy Week		
Death		
Resurrection		
Ascension		
Gift of the Holy Spirit		
Telling the world about Jesus		

2 Look at the diagram of the Christian year
Notice that there are colours marked in each of the boxes. These are the colours worn by the priest (his vestments, illustrated on the right) and of the cloths covering the altar and lectern in the Roman Catholic and Anglican churches during that season.

Choose one of the seasons of the year, and design a complete set of vestments with the correct colours for the season.

3 Which season is it now?

Find out what Sunday it is next. It will probably have a name like 'the tenth Sunday after Pentecost', or 'the second Sunday in Advent'. Use a Roman Catholic Missal or an Anglican Alternative Service book or lectionary to find out what Bible readings and prayers are set for next Sunday. The special prayer for that Sunday, called the Collect, is very often the key to what the rest of the readings are about, so read it carefully.

4 Now answer these questions

a Write down the references for the Bible readings.

b What is the Gospel about?

c Rewrite the Collect in your own words.

d. What is the main theme running through these readings which links them all together?

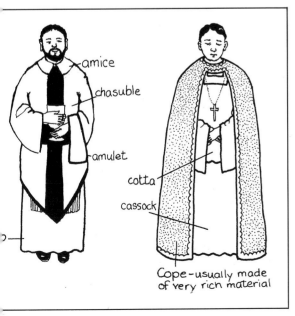

amice

chasuble

amulet

cotta

cassock

Cope – usually made of very rich material

5 Either

Imagine you have been invited to give a *two-minute* radio talk, called 'Thought for the Day'. Use the Bible readings which you have just examined to record a short talk based on the theme of these readings.

Or

Imagine you are a writer on the staff of a magazine. You have been asked to write a short religious article which will be helpful to your readers. Use the main theme from the readings you have examined to help you to do this.

6 For discussion

a Do you think it is helpful to Christians to celebrate the main events of the life of Christ as important festivals?

b Why do you think that the Church's year revolves around the life of Christ?

D An image of Christ

CHURCH ATTENDANCES

Here are some statistics. They come from an Anglican Church in a small town. The number of members refers to adults over the age of 16 who have entered their names on a list of church members called the 'electoral roll'. The numbers of attendances at services are for the main Sunday service. They refer to the number of people in the congregation who received Holy Communion.

7 Look carefully at the bar chart showing church attendances Then answer the following questions.

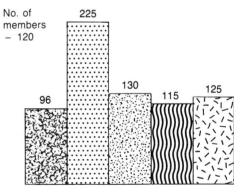

Church attendances

No. of members – 120

225

96 130 115 125

Average Sunday Christmas Easter Pentecost Harvest

a How many members are there?

b On which occasions are there more people attending the service than there are members of the church?

c Which is the most popular time to attend church?

d What reasons can you think of for the Harvest Service being a popular occasion, especially in country areas?

TIME FOR PREPARATION

Advent is the season of preparation for **Christmas**. Advent Sunday is the fourth Sunday before Christmas. The time of preparation for Christmas really begins, however, on the ninth Sunday before Christmas.

WAITING FOR THE MESSIAH

Christians prepare for Christmas by looking carefully at the way in which the people of Israel were prepared for the **Messiah**.

For centuries, the Jews had been expecting a special leader who would be God's messenger to Israel. His job was going to be to put the law of God directly into the hearts and minds of people so that they would want to do God's will. By the time of Jesus some of the Jews expected the Messiah to be the person who would free the Jewish people from the Roman occupation, and lead the Jews into a privileged position in the world. They expected him to be a political and military figure, as well as being a member of the royal family of David.

TWO THOUSAND YEARS OF PREPARATION

In preparation for Christmas, the Church looks at key points in the history of Israel. There is a feeling of growing excitement as, Sunday by Sunday, the main points of this great drama unfold.

Beginning with **creation**, God is seen to be at the centre of everything. He is seen as the creator and supporter of life. However, people have the free will and the desire to go their own way instead of God's way, and **sin** (the desire to do something when you know it is wrong) takes its place in an otherwise perfect creation. One man, Abraham, symbolizes

those who are prepared to be obedient to the will of God, and his faith is held up as an example.

The people of Israel became slaves in the land of Egypt. The Bible readings for Advent show Christians how God led them back into the promised land of Israel, with Moses as their leader. These readings demonstrate the Jewish and Christian belief that God acts within historical events. Other readings point to God's promises that he will continue to look after his people, even though some of them sometimes think that they are the only people left who believe in God. The Elijah story in 1 Kings 19, on the sixth Sunday in Advent, is taken as an example of this attitude.

Advent Crown

A NEW KING!

God's promises of help for the people of Israel are the theme of further Advent readings. Then comes the promise of a new king, who will be a descendant of King David who was the greatest king that Israel ever knew.

Suddenly, Christians are confronted with the exciting and explosive personality of John the Baptist, whose job it is to prepare the way for the new king. The countdown to Christmas is on. The new king is more than a promise, he is on his way, and Christians are expected to 'rejoice greatly'. Then, in the quietness of the night, comes Christmas Eve, and once more Christians are filled with joy, as they remember the birth of Jesus.

LIGHT

Light is another theme of Advent. Jesus called himself the 'light of the world'. Advent is a preparation for the coming of that light into the world. Some churches present this symbolically by using an Advent Crown. This consists of a wreath of evergreen in which there are four candles around the circle, and one central candle. On each of the four Sundays from Advent Sunday until Christmas an extra candle is lit, until all four are alight around the circle, leaving only the central candle to be lit at Midnight Communion on Christmas Eve. This symbolizes the coming of Christ, the 'light of the world'.

NOTES/DATABASE

Look up the following words in the glossary. Then use the definitions to make suitable entries for your notebook or database.

Advent	Christmas
Creation	Messiah
Sin	

Exploring
Christianity

Worship and Festivals

Gwyneth Windsor
and John Hughes

HEINEMANN
EDUCATIONAL

Heinemann Educational,
a division of Heinemann Educational Books Ltd,
Halley Court, Jordan Hill, Oxford OX2 8EJ

OXFORD LONDON EDINBURGH MADRID
ATHENS BOLOGNA PARIS MELBOURNE
SYDNEY AUCKLAND SINGAPORE TOKYO
IBADAN NAIROBI HARARE GABORONE
PORTSMOUTH NH (USA)

First published 1990
94 95 96 11 10 9 8 7 6 5 4

British Library Cataloguing in Publication Data
Windsor, Gwyneth
  Worship and festivals.
  1. Christian church. Public worship
  I. Title II. Hughes, John III. Series
  264

ISBN 0 435 30273 6

Designed and produced by VAP Publishing Services, Kidlington, Oxon

Printed and bound in Spain by Mateu Cromo

Acknowledgements

Religious Studies Consultant: W. Owen Cole

Thanks are due to Roger Owen and Janey Graham for commenting on the manuscript.

The publishers would like to thank the following for permission to reproduce copyright material:
Prayers for Peace for the Prayer on p. 59; The Shaftesbury Society for the cartoon on p. 11; The World Council of Churches for the logo on p. 95.

Thanks are also due to the following for permission to reproduce photographs:
Andes Press Agency/Val Baker p. 60 (A); Andes Press Agency/Carlos Reyes pp. 4 (D), 7 (G,H), 9 (C), 16 (A), 17 (C,D), 21 (C), 26 (A), 27 (B), 44 (A), 45 (B), 60 (B), 67 (D), 71 (D), 75 (E), 83 (E,F); Associated Kent Newspapers Ltd. p. 10 (all); Barnaby's Picture Library pp. 4 (B), 12 (A), 34 (F), 62 (bottom right), 88 (A); The Bridgeman Art Library pp. 15 (G), 52 (A), 91 (C,D); Buckfast Abbey pp. 18 (F), 29 (D), 37 (C); CAFOD p. 95 (D); Camera Press p. 5 (E); J. Allan Cash Ltd. pp. 4 (A,C), 29 (C), 32 (A), 34 (E), 40 (B), 62 (bottom left), 79 (C), 84 (B); Celtic Picture Agency/M.J. Thomas p. 89 (B); Christian Aid p. 11 (right); Church Missionary Society p. 62 (top right); Crisis p. 59 (E); Format Photographers/Mullen p. 38 (D); Format Photographers/Brenda Prince p. 15 (E); Foto-Huber p. 68 (A,B); Sally and Richard Greenhill pp. 13 (C), 62 (top left); Sonia Halliday Photographs p. 36 (B); Sonia Halliday/Laura Lushington p. 77 (B); Robert Harding Picture Library pp. 12 (B), 19 (E), 32 (C), 34 (G), 40 (A,C), 74 (D), 84 (A); Hutchison Library pp. 7 (F), 8 (B), 16 (B), 28 (A,B), 36 (A), 41 (D), 43; ITC Entertainment Ltd pp. 47 (D), 64 (A,B), 65 (B), 72 (A,B), 74 (C); Network/Lewis p. 85 (C); Network/John Sturrock p. 56 (A); Chris Ridgers p. 39 (top); Salvation Army p. 58/59 (D); The Scout Association p. 13 (D); Scripture Union pp. 20 (A,B), 22 (D); Syndication International Ltd p. 56 (B,C); Topham Picture Source pp. 67 (E), 87 (D,E); Voluntary Service Overseas pp. 32 (B), 92 (A,B); Youth Hostels Association p. 93 (C); Zefa Picture Library (UK) Ltd pp. 33 (D), 45 (C), 54 (B), 55 (C,D), 64 (C).

All other photographs supplied by the authors.

Cover photograph by Zefa Picture Library (UK) Ltd/Janoud.

Every effort has been made by the publisher to obtain permission to reproduce copyright material and to acknowledge copyright holders. If any material is incorrectly attributed the publisher would be happy to make the necessary amendments.

CONTENTS

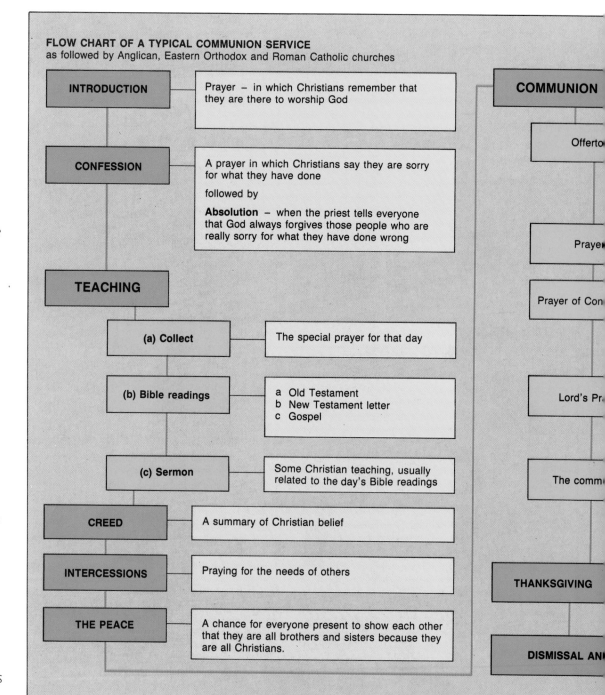

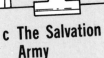